T0194250

The Other Shoe

Beyond Our Vows

Serenity Sole

WESTBOW PRESS

PRESS®

A DIVISION OF THOMAS NELSON
& ZONDERVAN

WestBow Press books may be ordered through booksellers or by contacting:

WestBow Press
A Division of Thomas Nelson & Zondervan
1663 Liberty Drive
Bloomington, IN 47403
www.westbowpress.com
1 (866) 928-1240

Because of the dynamic nature of the Internet, any web addresses or
links contained in this book may have changed since publication and
may no longer be valid. The views expressed in this work are solely those
of the author and do not necessarily reflect the views of the publisher,
and the publisher hereby disclaims any responsibility for them.

This book is a work of non-fiction. Unless otherwise noted, the author
and the publisher make no explicit guarantees as to the accuracy of
the information contained in this book and in some cases, names
of people and places have been altered to protect their privacy.

Any people depicted in stock imagery provided by Getty Images are
models, and such images are being used for illustrative purposes only.
Certain stock imagery © Getty Images.

ISBN: 978-1-9736-3098-2 (sc)
ISBN: 978-1-9736-3099-9 (e)

Library of Congress Control Number: 2018906883

Print information available on the last page.

WestBow Press rev. date: 6/29/2018

Introduction

It has taken me several years to write this book. This is my third attempt. Time affects how you see some things and I feel it's time to let it all go. It's starting at a specific "beginning," of course but out of fairness to you, the reader, I feel you must be forewarned. Although the book includes some gender-identity issues, it is written from my own point of view and I realize that others will have their own opinions as well. Some of the names have been changed from years ago since my memory fails me.

Although I may seem to straddle the line in some of the things that I will relate here, please know that I continue to believe that we are what we are. Nature has chosen our paths for us, but we have the responsibility to be the best we can be. We may not have a choice in our chromosomes, our hair colors, our genders, or our mental limitations, but we are responsible for our own attitudes, our goals, and ultimately, what we do with our lives. I believe science can change the spots on a leopard, but he will still be a leopard by nature.

As a teenager, I chose to seek a spiritual life so my own viewpoints and subsequent choices are based on my faith. I would never have married a woman, so my marriage was over as soon as I accepted the fact that my husband believed himself to be a woman. The pain of watching the man I loved go through the process of this physical change is almost beyond words. This book is my meager attempt to explain it from my "side". There are emotions that I still cannot express, but I know that it was no easier on my husband as he was driven by even more diverse emotions than mine. The key word here is "*acceptance*". I accepted it to the extent of toleration, which is not necessarily the same as approval. I accepted the fact that my husband believed himself to be female, and I accepted the fact that there was nothing I could do or say to change his mind. My approval or disapproval had nothing to do with it.

My mom always said there are at least two sides to every choice in life. I was encouraged to look at all possibilities when making decisions, and my dad even went so far as to make a pros and cons list. It often helped to visualize the different ways to look at something by looking at them on paper. When we are young, we rely on our parents and peers to guide us in the choices we make. People told my husband, Jay (not his real name), he was a boy as he had the necessary parts. He, therefore, grew up as a boy.

Should you choose to continue reading, please read with an open mind and do not judge too harshly. Gender issues have come to the forefront in recent years. We hear about it on television and you read about it in national magazines. Believe me: it's very challenging when it's your own family, when it's people you directly live with and care about. Change is inevitable in life, and how you handle change shows the kind of person you are. Live life to the fullest, but live responsibly, knowing that others are always watching and learning from you. We will be held responsible for our own choices in life. Let's begin.

1

Happiness is a point of reference. I'm single, alone and I'm happy - not all the time, but, on the whole, I'm happy. In the eyes of the law, I am divorced, but in my own eyes, I'm a widow. Life hasn't always been like this. Thinking back over my experiences and circumstances is like turning the pages of a book. It just depends on where you start the story and the viewpoint it gives you. It's making me feel pretty old right now! Honestly, if I have to find a point of beginning, it would have to be with the high heel, lavender shoes that I got for my 23rd birthday from my husband. They were gorgeous, and they perfectly matched the chiffon dress, which I also received. The thing is, they were actually two left shoes. This seems a pretty good example of my married life at times. My recollections from the past haven't changed. However, how I choose to apply them and put them introspectively into my life has changed. Part of the reason for this book is so that I can move past any remaining bitterness I still carry and get on with whatever life holds for me. I can only speak for myself - there is hope.

It may be helpful for you to know a bit more about my upbringing in order to put what you read into the proper perspective. I don't think I've ever perceived myself as being perfect, but I must admit that I do not have two left feet either. I may be a klutz at times, and I certainly did my fair share of falling during gymnastic events, but it's not because I had two left feet. Really!

Speaking of gymnastics, I actually joined the high school team in order to "catch up" on my skills and sports lingo. Since I grew up in a true three room country school, we did not have "physical education" as such. We had recess, which included baseball in the sand-burr infested lot behind the school, jump rope on the dirt in front of the building, dodge ball against the side of the school (when we had a ball), red rover and various games of tag.

We did have one slide which was a very tall, hazardous, thing that was treacherous to climb in the winter but gave you a satanically wild ride down. Of course, some kids would chicken out at the top and create chaos trying to come back down the ladder. Usually, there would be three or four students lined up behind them, ready to go down, so bailing out was not an option. Since it was made of shiny metal, it also got really hot on sunny days. You really earned your wings on that thing; you also learned who your friends were!

We also had a teeter-totter for a while. We could actually get three kids on each side of it. Unfortunately, we also learned how to jump off, spilling unsuspecting riders crashing to the ground. Fortunately, we did not have that many kids in school so word got out pretty quickly. Woe to any new students!

We had monkey bars erected when I was in the big room (4th through 6th grade) and someone broke their arm the first week they were up. Of course, Dwight and Deb got their heads smashed with a baseball bat during recess, so nothing was ever really safe. Boy, did we laugh when Dwight's hair grew between the bandages on the back of his head. It looked like a spider web! I myself had to have stitches to repair a hole in my knee when I fell over some barbed wire in the woods (also on the playground). Most of the time, we were left to our own devices for recess. We learned to sink or swim, get along or get left out. It was life at its fullest!

The merry-go-round was the best though. It was a metal one with tall handles on the end of it. It was the kind that was easy to push and jump up on. I held the record, for a short while, for being on it the longest without getting tossed off, or throwing up. Looking back, it seemed much bigger than it actually was. Even now I get dizzy at the thought of it.

Our mid-west area was full of country schools during the 60's. School districts were still being mapped out and several of the small, nearby lakes, were the last to be claimed by the townships. Our school had a large basement which housed the kindergarteners, and the two rooms upstairs divided the 1st through 6th grades (three in each room). Yup, the teachers taught three grades in the same room. It actually worked out pretty sweet for many students who were able to either work ahead, or needed the reinforcement of lower lessons. Many years ago, this school actually went through 12th grade! Our transportation was usually one of our parents picking everyone up on the way to school. My mom had a convertible car that she could really jam kids into. Her car, by design at that time, had only one seatbelt in the back, and it reached from one side of the car to the other. We actually had six kids pinned under it at times, and several on laps in the front seat. Thankfully, she always tried to pick the smallest ones to be on top. Granted, the school was only two miles from our home but you sure couldn't do that today.

Some of my fondest memories in life are of that old school house, and my best friends, even now, share those same memories with me. The big room had paneling on the lower half of the walls so our "right" of passage, when we reached 6th grade, was putting personal notes between the cracks in the wall. They were notes of anger, love, and promise. The school is still standing, but it's been turned into a home. I always wondered if the owners had found all of the notes we had stuck in the wall when they remodeled the building.

They even removed the cool, metal, emergency stairs that came down from the side of the schoolhouse from the younger room. Although I forget who it was that got their tongue stuck on it in the winter one year, I sure remember the mass pandemonium that followed. We had a huge lesson in first aid from the fire department that day. I'm sure I saw one of them smiling wickedly as they applied the cold, running water to the steaming, frozen railing . . . and tongue. We were mesmerized as we watched the red water running off and heard the blood curdling screams.

From that grade school, I continued my education in the school district's junior high school. Although there were six students in my entire 6th grade class - there were probably thirty students in my first class alone in 7th grade. I was overcome to say the least. I never dreamed there were that many kids in the world, let alone just in the 7th grade. I vomited in my home room class that first day from nerves. That's the day I met Brooke. She helped me clean up the mess on the floor. I never knew her very well, but I'll always be grateful for how she saved me on the first day of school, and took me under her wing. Apparently, she had several brothers and sisters at home and was used to helping "clean up the messes." Lucky me!

School life gradually got a smidgen better although I was always feeling a bit shy, and I didn't take part in any clubs or "clicks" within the students. Since my sister was already in high school, I felt alone and totally lost in such a big building. In grade school, I had always felt a bit like *queen of the school* since there wasn't much competition by other girls - nothing too self-proclaiming about that is there? After all, I was the only girl in my 4th and 5th grade classes. Physically, I was great at sports; my grades were good. I truly enjoyed all of the outdoor adventures we invented on the playground, many of which came from my own imagination (we collected rocks and pretended we were horses, among other things). In junior high, I was definitely on the bottom of the pond. My emotionally redeeming quality was music.

Back in my 6th grade year, we were introduced to the Orchestra. A music director came into our country school, and let us try various instruments hoping to recruit members to the band or orchestra in junior high. Although I had played piano since I was six, and could read music pretty well, this was the first hands on I'd ever had concerning other instruments. It was recommended that I would play the flute or the violin. I'm not sure how that decision was made, but I chose the violin. I think it may have had something to do with the new girl. She was the sixth person in my 6th grade class (the second girl). She created quite a stir since she was from a bigger city and was quite pretty. It turned out that she played the violin, and I was enthralled with it. I was hooked.

Now, the violin is not an easy instrument to play, and it was not an easy instrument to listen to all by itself . . . at least not when *I* played. My dad loved to hear us play piano, but my mom was the one who supported my choice in the violin since she had some experience in her past. I truly appreciated her patience, because I learned enough during that summer to be accepted into the orchestra in 7th grade. I still have my violin – testament to my motivation and joy of the instrument.

My musical abilities also led me to vocal performance. Now, I had used my piano skills at the elementary level, and would play and lead songs for the rest of the kids on rainy days in the basement of my country school. However, when the teacher told me to stop singing and play louder (I was horrified!), I took it to mean I didn't have a very good voice. Also, I had broken my nose at an early age. I ran into a tree (klutz), nothing to do with shoes, and I rationalized that it wasn't the nicest sounding voice around. Therefore, I was thrilled when I made it into the choir, as well, as an alto. There, I met my most favorite teacher, Mr. D. If ever there was a teacher who loved his job, it was Doc and he showed his love of it through his teaching. He could truly make the day better with his jokes and infectious laughter. Since choir was considered an elective, it wasn't everyone's first choice. He made music FUN and he had the ability to inspire even the worst of us. He was that good!

2

It was during my junior high years that I also met Marie, still one of my closest friends. Of course I didn't like her then. Unlike Jackie, my next door neighbor, whom I thought of as a sister (even though she threw rocks at me when she was three), Marie chose me to be her friend and proceeded to stalk me for years. I was terrified of her because she was outgoing, and I was not. She was loud and crazy, and I was not, although I admit I had it in me. Somehow she knew that we were more alike than I did. So, she kidnapped me in her green Volkswagen beetle one day, and gave me a ride home. She wheedled her way into my life. God bless her!!

It was Marie who, as freshmen, talked me into joining the gymnastics team in order to "catch up." Being from a country school, I didn't even know what *bombardment* was. We just called it dodge ball. I was unfamiliar with terms and rules. Although I was quite athletic, I stuck out like a sore thumb when directions were given. Under her tutelage, I became a contender in tumbling, free exercise, and vaulting. Of course that was before there were foam mats for the floor, and shin splints were a daily issue. She was the team manager and saved me from many tense moments of injury and embarrassment. I learned to laugh at myself more. I also learned not to be on the opposing side when we played *bombardment*. She was a power house and left welts on people when she threw the ball. Girls actually cried when they had to stand against her! I was extremely glad to be on her side.

It turns out that Marie and I were rather equally matched. She offered me friendship and guidance; she really listened to me when I needed to talk and didn't always give an opinion. I helped her with other things. Particularly, she was a terrible speller (sorry but it's the truth), and I'd proof her work. Even in college, she let me double-check her papers for spelling errors. We would probably be called nerds now, not that we were extremely smart, but we seemed to fit in with that bunch the best. Some of our friends were REALLY smart . . . like Valedictorian smart! I'm not sure what they saw in us but we were a close knit bunch nonetheless.

Marie was also talented musically, so she joined the orchestra as well. We sat side by side playing second violin through junior high, senior high and even junior college. She remains a dear friend, and now works as a bus driver for the same school district where I work. We share the same love for those with special needs and I truly admire her upbeat attitude.

Before I received that ill-fated pair of lavender heels, and before I was married, my favorite shoes were cowboy boots or tennis shoes. I never liked going barefoot, and I always stubbed my toes when wearing flip flops on my bicycle. Sometime in junior high, it was also discovered that one of my legs was shorter than the other. I started wearing a short lift in one shoe, which made it difficult to find the right shoes. Heels were always a challenge.

The reason I needed to catch up on my gym lingo was due to the fact that I was in both the orchestra and choir during my junior high years. The administration kept saying that I had to take PE/Gym class, but the music teachers wouldn't give me up. That was fine with me for two reasons. One, I absolutely loved my music classes and two, I was absolutely terrified of the PE teacher! She had a really loud voice and not much patience. I felt very stupid in her presence.

I was totally unaware of any social status, which put me in a league of my own. In 8th grade, a fellow student casually walked by me in the hall, and commented upon how I'd finally found a dress that went above my knees. I looked down and realized there was a world out there I had no knowledge of. I remember as a kid, asking my mom one day, "Hey mom, what does sex mean?" I was on the couch reading at the time, while my mom and older sister were at the kitchen counter. She and my sister looked at each other before she carefully responded. "Well," she started out, "it means when boys and girls grow up and get married" . . . and I stopped her. "No, no . . . what does it mean when it says, sex: male or female?" It had something to do with the questionnaire I was reading at the time and my mom gave a BIG sigh of relief. Now, that question was years before 8th grade, but it shows how simple gender issues were back then. Jackie showed me in a book that her mom was reading, about what happened when people had sex. Jackie was 2 years younger than me. My mom had always thought, with all my animals, I would have figured the sex thing out. I guess I was a bit slow. I just couldn't see what all the fuss was about.

But that is a reflection of the short comings of my self-image as well. Perhaps my years at the country school helped emphasize the fact that what we wore didn't really matter – at least to me. We didn't have the huge peer factor of what was "in" for our wardrobe. We all wore hand-me-downs and were happy when something actually fit. New shoes were something to be celebrated! We didn't have a local mall to hang out at. A big treat for us was to be able to go to town and get ice cream or maybe hotdogs at the local corner stand. The kids in my neighborhood would ride our bikes to play tennis at a local school or simply around the lake for something to do. At one point during my junior high years, I remember my mom facing me into the bathroom mirror and asking me if I really didn't care what I looked like. Keep in mind that it was the time of big bouffant hair and our moms were all competing on who could get their own hair the highest. I felt that there were more important things to worry about than my hair style. Granted, my hair was a bit shaggy but I saw nothing wrong with it. Having now worked in a middle school, which is the same as junior high, I think a lot of students are misjudged by their appearance. Sometimes our internal struggles to find ourselves take time. Life was full, even without all of the electronic gizmo's that demand attention now days. I was a middle child and sometimes felt neglected between the baby boy, and the older sister. Somewhere between me and my brother (7 years), my mom had a miscarriage. I remember my dad, at the time, saying how much he wanted a son. In fact, until my brother was born, I wanted to be a boy because I knew my dad wanted a son. I was the gofer, the peacemaker, the babysitter, the punching bag, the listener, the doormat . . . all of the above. Having worked in the educational system for many years now, I believe that middle children are usually better rounded. They've experienced life as the youngest and somewhat as the oldest as well. I was truly a dreamer, but I was blessed in so many ways! I admire my parents so much for the values they gave us kids. Making ends meet was as difficult then as it is now. My dad struggled in the business world to keep a step ahead, and my mom eventually worked for him in the property management field. Although she worked for the telephone company when my folks got married, mom stayed home until my brother was old enough to look after himself. My sister was also the built in babysitter. Mom took great pride in studying and passing the necessary tests to assist in my dad's company. My folks were very generous and gave our family many opportunities to participate, play and share in life. They taught us how to play tennis and went for bike rides with us. My mom was in charge of the Witches Cave every year at the school's carnival. I came away from childhood with a profound respect of family and church. I was also surrounded by nature, the greatest teacher. I've often said that I had the best childhood in the world!

3

It may sound kind of strange but I liked animals a lot more than I liked most people. That's the truth. At present, I teach nature, arts and crafts during the summer for the local community education program. I take great pleasure in seeing the look of intense rapture on children's faces as they discover the joy of holding a turtle or snake in their hand. The environment of the world is changing and kids don't have the same opportunity to play in the mud, catch fireflies, walk in the rain on a dirt road and see how pretty the rocks are when they are wet. Granted, it's not the thing for everyone, but I feel the things of nature can teach us about life sciences in a great productive and fun way. My education in nature was a gift of growing up and I tell students about my own experiences to make points.

My folks allowed me to collect, own, trade and buy different kinds of animals. This is an attraction which still calls to me today. From my first pet, a lizard named Millie Kay, that I inherited from a friend in grade school, to horses in the garage, I kept any animal I could get my hands on. Since we lived on a lake, that also included the resident turtles, frogs, snakes, bullheads (catfish), crayfish, and ants to name a few. I had a wonderful childhood learning lessons in nature from nature. In fact, I have to mention the rodents.

My aunt received a pair of mice as a gag gift one year. She was terrified of them! Well, my mom, bless her heart, let me keep them. They were supposed to be both boys and were harmless but I had to change Ernie's name to Ernestine when she gave birth to 5 babies. I began raising more rodents for a while after that. I enjoyed watching the interactions of the family units and took some as a project to the local 4H fair. I laughed so hard when the babies were learning to use the exercise wheel. They'd all pile on the wheel and then the mom would get on and send them all flying in different directions. What a hoot! Mice are lots of fun to raise, until they start eating each other, but let's not go there. Additionally, a friend of mine asked me to keep her white lab rat for the summer. I joyfully accepted although my mother hesitated over the tail, and I was off and running again. I raised rats for years, and bred them for different colors. My favorite one was Munchkin. He was a black and white hooded rat and was clever. Somehow, he would sneak out of his cage at night, and loved to run up and down the piano keys in the den. Unfortunately, the den, where the animals and the piano were, was right below my parents' bedroom. My dad would come storming into the bedroom that my sister and I shared and yell, "Your rat is loose again!" He did not like getting woken up in the night and losing sleep over that rat. Of course, *he* refused to put him away. We had a great respect for dad and his authority.

There were other occasions where he felt the need to yell as well. But nothing hurt me as much as his cold, hard, stare. As a parent, I've learned that different "deeds" deserve different punishments and as a para-professional, I've learned that cause and effect can vary for different people as well. Unfortunately, I've been told that I have the same, hard look. Apparently, I use it to show my displeasure when things don't go the way I think they should (sorry!). On the flip side though, my dad was my champion. When the neighbor took a sledge hammer to a wild rat in his garage, I was there . . . pulled in by unseen arms to watch the horrible massacre. I don't even remember running home through the tears, but I do remember the sheltering support of my dad as he held me through my blubbering torrent. He showed his true grit later in life - my dad was a great man.

I also loved to read romance novels which didn't always fit in with what everyone else was doing. Jackie would actually hide my book so that I would have to come outside to play with her. Pretty sad considering I'd give anything now to be able to walk next door and visit with her. We live near each other, but life has certainly changed the close companionship of youth.

Jackie has always been one of my best friends. We lived next door to each other and she's the one who threw rocks at me when I was 5, but I forgave her. I'm the one who accidently bumped her with my knee on her eyebrow while we were horsing around on an inner-tube in the lake. It swelled her eye shut almost instantly and turned her eye gazillion different shades of purple . . . but she forgave me. Jackie was there when my first foal was born and we competed side by side at the local 4H fairgrounds.

Actually, I can't list all the fun things we've been part of together. She is my chosen sister and there's not many memories that don't include her. She had to have a horse when I finally got one. With the onslaught of equine things, we joined the local 4H program and thereby sealed the deal of my interest with horses and kids. We went to horse shows, fairs, parades and joy rides. We learned about archery, outdoor cooking, gardening (we had gardens side by side) and many more project areas.

At times I was extremely jealous of her since everything she had seemed to be better than mine, but she kept me honest and humble. We've been through thick and thin. We were in each other's weddings, the birth of our children, and the passing of both of our fathers. She helped keep me on keel when my own marriage was dissolving.

We learned to fight, to share, to listen, to ignore, to laugh and to cry together . . . after all, it was Jackie who finally taught me the facts of life. Ha!

There were the usual really cute boys in school, and I'd follow them around the halls with my girlfriends, but I never really dated through high school. Oh, I did the "sock hops" at school as a social event, but seldom had the courage to dance. Besides, there were pretty strict rules about what kind of dancing was allowed in school back then. Our group would do group dances almost like the line dances of today.

Several of my other friends were also in 4H. In case you are unfamiliar with 4H, there is a pledge that we adhere to: "I pledge my **head** to clearer thinking, my **heart** to greater loyalty, my **hands** to larger service and my **health** to better living for my club, my community, my country and my world". That's a pretty high standard to live by. We had some great leaders who were a big influence on us. We tended to follow the rules and supported each other in the choices we made. Of course, the choices back then were more like: smoke or not, length of your skirt, go to the game or not, swear or not, where to sit at lunch to see the cutest boys, what movie was coming out, and who's dad/mom was driving. The drugs and sexual issues facing kids today weren't even thought of. We did things as a group; we'd gather in the back of a pickup to go to the local drive-in theater or mall (there was only one). The group of kids around the lake would get together at night and play Marco Polo or tag by the moonlight. Boy, we sure couldn't get away with that now! It had never occurred to us then, that there could be dangerous people behind the trees just looking for opportunities to hurt us. We were more afraid of our parents than of anything bad happening. When our parents flashed the outside lights on and off, we knew we'd better beat it home right away or suffer the consequences.

It was definitely a more trusting time, a safer and more fun time. There were no video games, computers, cell phones, etc. We did our daily chores and played outside. Well, I do remember when the bigger kids of the neighborhood came over one night and mud-balled the side of our house when my folks weren't home. I think it was friends of my sister but I didn't tell because I didn't know their names . . . well, that was the excuse that I used when my folks got up the next day and saw the house. I wasn't a snitch!

My aunt once commented to me that I was an easy pushover. For example, if we were visiting my cousins and someone wanted something from the refrigerator, I was generally the one to get up and go get it for them. I hadn't really thought about it much before that comment from her, but she was right. I had a hard time saying *no* to people. I think I just didn't like to disappoint anyone; I was a good kid. It made me feel good to think I was helping people. My mom always told me that if I wanted to be a doormat, someone would always walk on me. I realize now, as an adult, that even my mom would take advantage of this weakness in me at times. She is a very smart lady. I truly think that everything I needed to learn in life, I learned from my mom, sometimes better late than never. That includes the basics of music, psychology, philosophy, science, art, and theology. She loved my dad and stood by him through prosperity and the potholes of life, and taught me what commitment was. At this time in my life, I'm still not sure how she did it. She was a model for me so that when my marriage and life fell to ruin, I could survive.

I think the key to all challenges in life is love. Unfortunately, that word seems to have many different meanings to as many different people. Our family wasn't perfect and my folks had challenges in their marriage which we weren't always privy to. My parents always worked it out. They sought out help when needed and weren't afraid to admit mistakes. They taught me that life isn't fair . . . deal with it. I've also come to the conclusion that fair, is not the same as equal.

There are explanations for the choices we make. I try not to use excuses because they are unproductive words. Explanations can clear up confusion in actions and words. They can be flexible and can bridge the gap of communication. I feel that I have an ability to feel empathy towards others . . . or maybe I just try to take time to understand what someone else is feeling. I care. It is my nature to be giving and that has gotten me into trouble at times. There have been times that my caring about someone has been misinterpreted. One of my riding students became so attracted to me that he was almost stalking me. When I assisted him during a riding lesson, as I was trained to do, he took it as my personal interest in him. He started coming to the church services where I attended. He called our home at various times every day. At that time, I had a new baby and we were building our home. I ended up attending a meeting with him and his counselor, in order to convince him that his infatuation was one sided and I was feeling harassed. Apparently, I was part of a long list of women that he had attached himself to. Jay was very supportive of me as I dealt with this sensitive issue, but was equally grateful when the calls ended and normal life resumed. I also tend to root for the underdog. I've been one myself several times in life, and I truly believe there have been angels helping to pull me through. There you go - love.

I'm sorry to bore you with so much of my past, but as I reflect on the present, the past seems to have directed my responses to events along the journey. I guess there *is* something about the saying that we are products of our environment, at least to a point.

5

By the way, those two lavender, high heel shoes were on sale and couldn't be returned or exchanged. My husband, somehow, convinced the salesman to exchange one shoe. It took a lot of fancy talking because that clerk did not want to get into trouble by accepting a "return". I guess he finally realized that he had 2 right shoes that he was not going to be able to sell, and that we would not leave without the correct pair. That is a perfect example of the type of character my husband was. His persistence was a gift! I would be able to wear my new shoes after all. He would not take no for an answer . . .

I met Jay when I was 20 and working part time for my dad's company. Although dad had his own realty offices, he worked for a bank as well. I would be working in the gift shop, or the parking booth collecting tickets and money, or cleaning offices . . . pretty much anywhere I was useful. My college classes were up the hill from the building where I worked. Jay was working in the basement of the same building. When I worked in the gift shop, Jay and his friends would sit across the hallway in the cafeteria at lunch time and watch me through the glass. Although it was a bit flattering at first, it really bothered me. I thought they were laughing at me. I wasn't used to being the object of attention and I was much more comfortable in a group. I just couldn't understand his interest in me. I didn't wear makeup because I had bunches of allergies, and I wasn't a great dresser (some things never change). There were a few guys from high school that I kept in touch with, and I wasn't trying to attract anyone. During our married life, I often felt that I wasn't good enough for Jay because he always seemed to be trying to change me, to improve me which wasn't necessarily a bad thing. The way it was done just made me feel like I wasn't good enough just being myself. Like the salesman, I had a hard time saying no to him. I wonder, now, if Jay saw me more as a Barbie Doll, more like what he wished *he* could be.

I'd been asked out on dates before; a few boys were interested in me at school. However, by the time I had thought about it, tried to hash out my feelings, it would be too late! There were also the boys that were great friends, and I didn't want to spoil the friendship by dating. I was all about the "prince charming" kind of guy (see, I did read too much) and often thought long term, instead of the short term fun associated with dating. It seems that, one by one, my group of girlfriends was dissolving and getting married. Actually, I was a bit afraid of boys and felt unsure of what dating was all about. Also, there were always rumors and stories about what happened on dates. I tended to learn things from watching my older sister, and I was afraid to go out on my own. My social education was lacking. Therefore I was really confused and angry with myself for lacking confidence as a young adult. See . . . explanation of choices, but not excuses!

Jay kept asking me out and I kept saying no. He finally downright lied to me and said that his family was moving to Nashville because his mom had cut a record. This was my last chance to go out with him and he wouldn't take no for an answer. He said he would pick me up at 7:00 . . . and I was there. Well, his mom really had cut a country record but there were no plans of moving to Nashville. Jay was quite proud of himself for tricking me and loved telling everyone how clever he was. Truth be known, I loved his parents almost immediately. They were so different than mine. I lived in the country yet they called themselves urban cowboys. They played country music, which I really learned to love, while I played classical style in orchestra. We were complete opposites yet there was definitely an attraction there.

6

Communication is the key to almost every conflict I can imagine. I'll bet you've heard *that* before. It may not actually solve anything, but I have found that if I take the time to listen, I may learn something. If I learn something, I may be able to adjust my opinion or at least make more sense of the conversation. Perhaps the confusion is just that everyone has something to say, but we don't always take time to listen to each other. My favorite line is: *say what you mean and mean what you say.* I try to stand behind what I say but not everyone else has the same ideals. I'm not very good at small talk and perhaps I'm a bit judgmental when people just seem to respond to each other with non-committal remarks. I also feel that actions speak louder than words. Unfortunately, I've been known to fall short of my own ideals. I'm still growing in the art of communication.

Because I was a quieter voice, my husband tended to speak for me. As a kid, my mom did most of my talking for me so I guess it's not too surprising that I allowed Jay to basically take over decision making. I tended to keep my feelings inside. I had headaches quite often growing up, and my mom said I gave them to myself. Personally, I often blamed them on my broken nose (ran into a tree – barefoot, no shoes) but I've since discovered they come with cold fronts as well.

People seemed to come out of the woodwork with advice when they learned I was going out with Jay. Some of the people he worked with actually warned me to wear my seatbelt. He had a LOT of speeding points. I was so nervous about going on a date that I gave myself hives. I knew they were different than allergies because they were on my neck and chest, nowhere near the usual nose or face. I should have asked myself why I was so nervous around Jay, but I guess I was excited that someone was honestly interested in me. The fact that he also played guitar and sang, was a bonus to me. See, we did have some things in common! I quickly learned to love country music, and I felt comfortable bantering with Jay's dad about styles and rhythms. On the first date, Jay asked me what I would say if he asked me to marry him. Since I presumed he was kidding, I said I'd say "no way" and laugh at him. Well, he did and I did. There were not many dates that didn't end with this same exchange of "would you" and "no. It was kind of funny at first but it got rather old. It seemed more of a battle of wills instead of true emotions. Part of my hesitation was that Jay's friends and some family said that I looked just like his old girlfriend. And the fact that this girlfriend had died was just so unfair . . . was he seeing me or her? How could I compete with that? My lack of confidence in myself was definitely showing.

We dated for about a year. Although the question of our marriage got to be repetitive, life was always exciting around Jay. He actually tried to learn to like horses. Truthfully, he got dumped six times the first time we rode together. He said he was bucked off. I did note that the horse was standing still each time Jay came off but I let him tell his story his way. There are so many joyous memories of working together . . . building a hay barn, putting cars back together, pulling up trees to build fences, walking sick horses, always on an adventure of some kind. It seemed very difficult for Jay to just relax and do nothing. Life was full and I didn't complain. I was enjoying the ride.

Jay also played guitar and sang in his family's country band. I often accompanied Jay when he was playing a gig at night. Most of the jobs were in smoke filled bars which bothered my allergies a lot but I would dutifully go anyway. I would sit by myself or try to visit with other girlfriends and wives from the band. Since I'm not much good at small talk, I always felt uncomfortable in a bar. I'd watch all of the dancers (it seems everybody danced with everybody) although

I still was much too self-conscious to dance with anyone but Jay. He encouraged me to take my first drink. It seemed that's what everyone else did while enjoying the music and dancing. Eventually, they'd all get drunk so what's the fun in that? I must admit that I got drunk twice during that year of dating and couldn't understand why anyone would ever want to do that again so I chose not to drink. I chalked it up to being a learning experience. Besides, I was the designated driver after most gigs. There were also weddings where I would play piano and Jay would do a "special" song. He was always pushing me to play fiddle in his country band but I was not comfortable at playing by ear and I absolutely hated to be pushed into it. On the other hand, he did not read music. Looking back at it now, I think I should have been feeling tread marks on my back. Oh well, at the time it was all part of the fun and games of dating.

Because Jay was trying to fit into my life, I was trying to fit into his. He was a race car nut and he drove circle track whenever he could. He never had much money to put into his car but he and his dad were great backyard mechanics. His idea of a good time was to spend the evening working on his race car. I actually enjoy mechanical things myself so I didn't really mind spending time under the hood, holding the light so he could see. I actually learned a lot from that time of tinkering which helped me later in life when I had to fix my own vehicles.

It seemed that everything I learned to do, surprisingly became my job to do it. That may actually be normal in some marriages but that particular fact didn't dawn on me 'til much later in our life together. However, I learned that to get him to help me with something, I first had to start it and mess it up so he would have to come help me . . . two can play at that game!

My friends supported me with my choice of Jay. They kind of enjoyed the bickering and bantering between us. I was usually overruled by Jay on things to do or whom to visit. Most of my inner turmoil was the fact that I seemed unable to effectively speak my mind. That strength didn't come until later in life. Jay, I'm sure, took my silence as acceptance. He was always doing something; good or bad, it was exciting to be around him. I was so used to being the peacemaker, the one who would make do, that it was just easier, when push came to shove, to just go along with whatever the plan was. The man was the head of the household in the Bible as well. My folks were not extremely affectionate in public and I pulled away from being overly demonstrative as well. I loved the stolen moments of making out in a car but I tried to avoid those times that would physically tempt us too far – I believed Jay respected me. I knew that Jay loved me and I trusted him to take care of me. I loved Jay and the past has ultimately brought me to the present. I'm just so sorry for the vast reaching damage along the way.

Our courtship was not without conflict. My parents really didn't approve of Jay. He didn't have a great paying job and didn't have a lot of goals at that time. Call it mother's intuition, but my mom actually hated him. Again, we never really had a constructive conversation about the shortcomings of my boyfriend but she lost no opportunity to put him down. She even went so far as to show a picture of me and an old boyfriend at my wedding shower, saying didn't they make a better picture? The shower was at our home and the snapshot was not shown to everyone there, but I was shocked that she had done it. I loved Jay's parents, although they were very different from my own. Or maybe it was because they were different that I loved them so. My parents were in the business world. Jay's dad worked in a factory. I felt my parents were not being fair and gave me a curfew of midnight. After all, I was 20 years old and could certainly make my own decisions! Being a mom myself now, I can put myself in my mother's shoes and understand the worry that was there, but then, it simply put a wedge between my parents and myself. I didn't think that my parents trusted *me*.

I should add that Jay pretty much hated my mom just as much and would reciprocate insult for insult although always out of her ear shot. I appreciated the effort they both put forth, in my presence, to be civil to each other. In later years, Jay would add additional family members and friends to the list of people in his mind that only pretended to accept him. We had many an argument over his judgmental attitude. He felt he was always right - about everything. I learned it was sometimes better to keep my own opinions to myself.

I think I said "Yes" to the final marriage proposal out of sheer desperation. I felt my life was at a turning point and I was so tired of the constant barrage of, "Will you marry me?" I knew I loved Jay and I could see us together forever. I was also tired of trying to be the peacemaker between my mom and Jay. After I said yes, it was like the entire world held its breath, just for a moment or maybe that was just me. It sounds very melodramatic but at the time, it seemed like I was waiting for the other shoe to fall . . . wondering if the world was going to break into song or perhaps fall apart. Actually, nothing happened at all. Except, the question changed from will you, to when. When? **When??**

7

The day before I said "yes" was Jay's birthday and we were out late, celebrating the occasion and having the usual argument about marriage. Even before we were married, we would have this battle of wills, which I seldom won. One bitterly cold night, Jay angrily got out of my car with a spare tire, and rolled it a mile or more home saying he couldn't stay in the car with me. (I can't remember why he had a tire.) Jay had a hard time letting go of something . . . as I said, he always thought he was right. I didn't even know what we were fighting about, although I laughed at him at the time. He was very insistent about things back then. It became a bit more explosive later on, but then so did my own responses.

Jay did not always have a car to drive (mechanic, right?!) so I did a lot of the driving back and forth, something which my folks absolutely despised. I had a curfew of midnight which was sometimes hard to keep since we lived 40 minutes away from each other. Anyway, the night before I finally said "yes", I had an experience that changed my life. I had been baptized in our local church when I was much younger . . . I believed in Jesus and knew that I had been blessed in my life with so many things. However, on my way home that night, I was quite late and knew that my parents would be up waiting for me. I knew how bad the battle would be. The worst part of it all, was that I was ashamed at disappointing my parents by being so late. It was Jay's birthday and he had a hard time letting me go that night.

I was truly afraid to go home and I was crying in the car, praying to God for strength and composure. Jay's birthday is in January and the roads were snow covered and slippery. It was very difficult to see out the front window through the tears and as I came to a fork in the expressway, I felt out of emotional control. I was sobbing and talking to myself when I suddenly felt a soft, steady pressure on my right shoulder. Instead of giving me chills, it seemed to instill a calm, soothing, love. This sounds absolutely crazy, I know, but I actually looked in the rearview mirror to see who was in the back seat. No one was visibly there but I know what I felt. I was touched by the Spirit . . . I couldn't believe that God cared about me! I was unsure of why He made Himself known to me then, but I sang praises all the way home. If I concentrate, I can still feel the exact spot that was touched and I hold that memory in my heart. My parents were up and at the kitchen counter when I arrived home. I wanted to share my experience with them and I couldn't believe that I didn't even look different. I wanted to say to them, "Look at me!! Everything is going to be alright". Perhaps something did show, or perhaps it was just because I simply said I was sorry for keeping them up, and didn't argue with them. In any case, they simply shook their heads and went to bed. I know nothing for sure, except that I saw God in a very personal way that night. I haven't shared it with anyone except my dad on his deathbed. I had to tell him it was going to be okay and Jesus was real!

There was no revelation as to what to do or say about marriage during this comforting exchange in my car. I know that I had the utmost faith that God would be with me, no matter the choice. I guess that may be why I was so focused on what would happen when I said "yes" to Jay?!

8

I'm not sure that things actually changed after that. During the 1½ years of our engagement, my parents came to terms with the fact that I loved Jay. My mom helped me pick out my dress ($48) which needed a full slip ($52) and we got the veil at a going out of business sale ($2). It's not that my parents were cheap, it's more that I was easy. However, it was harder to find just the right shoes as Jay was just a tad shorter than me, so I had to have flats. I found just the right sandals and Jay found just the right platform dress shoes, so we looked perfect for the wedding pictures. My mom said that Jay had a "short person's" attitude, always acting like there was a chip on his shoulder. That may have been the case because as usual, our best laid plans needed to be revised; we had to change photographers a week before the wedding. Our scheduled photographer wanted to do pictures before the wedding, when we were all cleaner and fresher. He felt we'd have more opportunity to gather family and take our time with special shots before the service. Jay decided that he did not want to see me before the ceremony so we had to wait until after the ceremony for pictures. This, of course, delayed the time for the reception and inconvenienced some family members. My mother was furious. I, of course, simply went along with whatever Jay thought was best. He was leading. I was following. The reins had been officially passed.

Jay was laid off from his job before the wedding and my mom insisted that Jay be working when we wed. He found mechanics work to satisfy her and also because it was easy for Jay. He really was a great mechanic which he expanded on after our marriage. He obtained his Master Mechanics license and opened his own auto shop. Jay seemed to have a hard time working for someone else so it seemed to be the natural thing to do.

The other manipulation test my mom insisted on, was that I had to get certified as an instructor in therapeutic horseback riding before we got married. I had participated in a pilot program of Horseback Riding for the Handicapped (HRH) through our local cooperative extension service during the year of our engagement. I worked as a volunteer side-walker, leader, coach, groomer and anything else the program needed. Since I was deemed a "giver" by nature, this was a great fit for me. My mom offered to pay the bill, if I would go to the school and get certified as an instructor. She felt that it would be a possible backup plan for the future. What an opportunity!! Of course, since mom wanted me to, I didn't want to go and made every excuse I could because I was afraid. Although I truly admired the gal who was the instructor at my program, in my mind, she was everything I could never be. You had to be able to teach, talk, to be in charge, to delegate, to communicate, to organize . . . get the picture. In my mind, I could never do or be all those things. However, in order to get married, I had to go and try. (I still had a hard time saying "no" to mom!)

I loved the idea of animals and therapy. I had assisted a fellow student in high school with her patterning. Patterning is basically exercises that help stimulate the muscles and the mind into relearning physical tasks that you used to know. This student had been in an accident that left her in a coma. When she got back on her feet, they realized that she was challenged in certain physical areas. Therefore, I was able to be of service in her recovery. I admit that I liked helping her a lot and I learned enough about therapy that this work with HRH did have a lot of allure for me. However, my fears really held me back. Besides, if my mom wanted me to do it, I certainly didn't want to.

I like to think I was simply being a normal young adult in defying my parents, but it hit me quite late. I had watched my sister as an older teen go through a rebellious streak. It was heartbreaking to watch as control was challenged in every way my mom and sister interacted. I still had my horses so I was able to escape reality and spend time with my animals. But my sister was not bitten by the equine bug so she did not have a close distraction to divert confrontation. She had a lot of friends instead. I learned a lot from watching my sister and I'm amazed at how close we are today. As children, we went through various stages of hate and companionship. As adults, we have tried to be there for each other, even though we don't always see eye to eye. I appreciate the way she can see things from another point of view and isn't afraid to tell me her opinion. We may not always agree on how to manage a situation, but she has truly blessed me through her support and friendship.

My brother on the other hand, was the joy of my youth. I actually had him in mind when I wrote of all the things a middle child is. I grew from helping to change his diapers (he's seven years younger than me) to having to carry him home from the neighbors when he had a fit of temper. He eventually got his own horse and participated in 4H with Jackie and me. When we were children, he could do no wrong. As a young man, he tutored me for my first date with Jay (he said don't kiss him on the first date). My mom says I spoiled him. When he got married, Jay and I would visit their home and had a few traditions like making and decorating sugar cookies. He had a sarcastic sense of humor (like my dad) and he was a hoot to be around. He actually played on our softball team for years and I know that Jay thought of him as another brother. I know that the choices I made regarding how to handle the circumstances of Jay's identity crisis affected more than just myself, and I apologize to all who were hurt or felt mislead by those choices. Some family members, as well as friends, wrote us off when our marriage was dissolving around us. I believe they felt they were protecting their families from something they thought might be catching. I try not to be too judgmental as identity issues are such a personal matter. Friendship has its own boundaries of trust and I'm sure that many people felt their trust was violated. Even the simplest act of using a bathroom in the past with Jay, caused many disturbing memories for some people. I was also having some of these realizations so I could understand if some people chose to take a step away from us. Lost relationships are a constant sadness to me as our daughter and I have also lost the semblance of our family as a whole. At times, isolation started to bring about ideas of paranoia for me so how could I be critical of others? Since my brother and his wife had boys, we were not as close as my sister and her girls. They live near my sister and they remain close so I'm able to hear through the grapevine about life for them. He seems like a terrific husband and parent and I'm so proud of him for that!

I finished my training at the HRH (Horseback Riding for the Handicapped) site and was invited to take a temporary teaching position at an HRH program in an adjoining state. With the wedding so close, and everyone pushing me (Jay and my mom), I relented and accepted the position to teach for the summer after our wedding in May. My lack of confidence was pretty overwhelming at times. I had to reach pretty deep inside to face the duties of my job. My job included meeting new people, establishing the authority of being the new instructor, evaluating safety measures and instruction for handicapped individuals. However, I know that putting myself in that place of authority was a godsend. Apparently, my mom really did know me best because, although it was *very* difficult, I absolutely loved helping others share my joy of horses. In fact, I am still working part-time for an HRH program in my vicinity and can honestly say that I am the person I am today, because of what I have learned through working with others in the field. It wasn't an overnight growth but I started letting myself out more. I have been absolutely blessed to have been part of the program for so long. They (volunteers, parents, students and staff) have been my teachers, my inspiration, my sounding board, my critics, and my friends. If the good Lord has allowed me to be a tool in their lives, He has allowed them to be the hammer in mine. Believe me, the challenge has been a blessing and I know I receive more than I give.

Our wedding day was so beautiful! Since we had planned the service for Memorial Day weekend, we had anticipated that some guests would have other plans. In fact, we did not get very many reservations back so a few more guests were invited. It turned out that there was standing room only at the wedding. I remember looking down the row of bridesmaids, and smiling as I watched their bouquets shaking from nerves. Jay had had eye surgery just a week before the wedding. Somehow he had gotten a piece of metal in one eye and had to wear a patch over the eye allowing the cornea to heal. I was grateful that he took the patch off that day – I loved looking into his eyes while we said our vows. That part did make me nervous but I held his hands for strength and we came away a couple. I seemed to possess a calm that lasted all through the service and reception. The banquet facility had to add another table for the additional guests and the food was amazing. My parents had rented a beautiful rooftop restaurant to cater in fabulous food and one of my cousin's played music for dancing. We opened our gifts at the reception and although I refrained from a lot of dancing, Jay was having a great time on the dance floor. It was a joyous celebration with no undercurrents for the day.

We had reserved a hotel room for that night in a neighboring town. We had plans of driving to Kings Island the next day and I was anxious to see the Smokey Mountains. I'm not going to say much about our honeymoon except that I was totally unprepared for my wedding night and it took time for me to become accustomed to sleeping with someone else and learning about the marriage bed. I was unaware of the possibility of pain and Jay jokingly called me a prude. He was experienced about sex and couldn't wait for me to "catch up" with him, to explore. I admit that I must have been quite a disappointment at times but we learned to be patient with each other.

9

Between my experiences in the riding program, and my psychology classes in junior college, I began to grow within myself. I began to speak for myself. Unfortunately, a woman with opinions was not exactly what my husband had bargained for. Our relationship was strained at times in a battle of wills. But our love was still the cement that held it all together. As I began the process of "growing up", I began to question things I had taken for granted. Jay was very supportive in my efforts within the HRH program. He even took the time to help out in areas of repair on the farm. On the other hand, he was very unhappy that time working for HRH (exclusively on Saturdays) took my time away from him. He actually tried to volunteer for my classes but admitted that it wasn't his thing.

After my temporary position ended, we returned to our hometown and Jay began a business of his own. He opened an auto repair shop and put in twelve hours a day building clientele. I was able to run parts sometimes and helped clean the garage. Jay's shop was always busy - various people would stop by daily just to socialize which Jay accepted as word of mouth advertisement. Curiously, he even had a storage cupboard that he kept locked. When I asked about it, he stated there were things in there belonging to other people and he was safeguarding the contents for them. It was his version of a safe. I attributed that to the fact that Jay was a good friend. We had a great dog, Jasper, which stayed at the garage during the day but came home with us at night. I remember one night, sleeping with that dog on a rug in the shop, waiting for Jay to finish a car. We would sleepily watch as the mice came out and stole her dog food out of her dog dish. Those were busy, hectic, exciting days in our marriage. We were learning to rely on each other. I found work with an insurance company and maintained our home expenses while Jay handled all of the business expenses. I also found part time work with our local therapeutic riding program, the same one I initially volunteered at. Things were looking up!

My family seemed to come to terms with Jay. He had an infectious ability to motivate people. Although he made my dad a bit nervous, because he worked so fast, Jay was often called upon to help around the house. My dad was definitely not mechanically minded! Even my mom was won over with the fiasco of Quaker.

In the winter, our horses were kept across the street from my folk's house. In the summer, we moved them to a five acre site down the road which eventually became our own property. It had shelter and water and the horses loved it out there. Unfortunately, it was much more difficult to do the daily chores of feeding way out in the boonies.

Near Labor Day Weekend, about the 4th year after marriage, we made our evening trek to feed the horses. It was almost dark and when we threw the hay in, we noticed one of the horses was rolling. Now, a horse will naturally roll over to itch its back but this horse was constantly rolling, standing up and dropping down to roll again. This usually signifies a stomach ache that is called Colic in a horse. Horses that have colic have been known to roll over so much they actually twist their gut. It is a VERY painful way to die.

The only possible remedy we had available was to walk him. Quaker kept trying to roll so we had to keep him up, and it took both of us to do it. We had no way of knowing if he had already damaged his organs so we just kept walking him. There were no cell phones at that time and we knew that our vet would not be available until morning. It was *crazy* – no one knew we were out there and we could not leave to let anyone know. I still can't believe the resolve that Jay had. I loved that horse and Jay would not let it lie down and die. We walked that horse all night long, praying to stay awake, and praying it would keep walking. At times, we could take turns walking him around and around the field in the moonlight. Fortunately, it was a full moon and one of us could nap on top of the hill (it was cold!) while keeping an eye out for the coming pair so we could change leaders. It was a *very* long night but somehow, Quaker made it through. I felt really bad but at times we had to use a whip to get him back on his feet.

At daybreak, I drove back to my parent's house to let them know we were out there. They couldn't believe we'd been there all night! I returned to the field to take over from Jay. My dad actually showed up with lawn chairs and breakfast for us . . . my mom managed to get ahold of a veterinarian who made it out and put a gallon of mineral oil down Quaker's throat. The idea of this is to help loosen the blockage in the gut and help the horse eliminate it naturally. Our job was to keep walking the horse and check for sand in the feces. (That was Jay's job – he was a good sport about it, too!) Sand in the stools would indicate that the blockage may be breaking up. It was also an indication of the cause of the colic: sand.

We ended up missing work and we walked that horse for five days. If he wanted to stand, due to fatigue, we let him but whenever he tried to lay down, we walked him. My friend, Marie and her husband, came and put up a tent so we could rest whenever we could while they took over watching Quaker. My folk's kept us fed and we were fortunate that we could take the time off work. The vet ended up putting 3 gallons of mineral oil down that horse. He had recommended putting him down on the 3rd day but I swore I could hear sounds in his gut; he was eating and urinating. I just wasn't ready to lose him yet and Jay was as committed as I was. As it turned out, Quaker finally was able to pass the blockage. He had the worst case of sand colic the vet had ever seen. He lived another 20 years and it proved to my parents how devoted Jay was to me and the compassion he had for animals. Jay had surprised even me and it renewed my faith in him. He was my hero! Life had turned a corner and it proved much sweeter where my family was concerned.

10

We played softball several times a week, swam and played in the lake at my folks. Life seemed pretty good. I moved up in the insurance world, changing jobs a few times and we were saving what we could for a home and a family. Since I was always drawn to kids, I couldn't wait until we would have our own. Jay also wanted a big family but we waited while we built up the business and lead our very busy lives. Mom also kept reminding me how much children cost, and we should try to plan ahead for them. I actually used birth control for the first five years of our marriage, which certainly turned into a joke when I had fertility issues after that.

Anyway, I should also state that "I" was trying to save for future things because most of what Jay made, went right back into the business. Jay provided "fun" money and always wanted to go to the movies and out to eat. Now, part of that was the fact that I was not a very good cook, and part of that was Jay just liked the movies. I think the movies were a way that he could escape his life and get into roles that he always wanted to find himself in. He was so busy with work, that he truly enjoyed the plots in other people's lives. I always felt that if Jay had a college education, he'd be dangerous. In retrospect, I know that some money Jay was making, was not reported on any invoices. He always seemed to have side jobs he was working on. He also had a secret that he kept from me for over 26 years. It was that secret that, unknowingly, contributed to most of our conflicts in life.

I am not trying to make Jay out to be the bad guy here. It's almost impossible to make someone else change . . . making changes has to come from within ourselves. I always thought that marriage was supposed to be two people merging into one path. The path may not always be straight or easy, but there is a give and take that must be respected if you want to be able to maintain a good relationship. I think communication is the number one challenge in a marriage and in life. Jay and I physically worked very well together but we never communicated well. I felt I was trying but Jay wasn't listening or didn't care. Both of those things are hurtful on any terms and I'm sure that Jay would say the same about me. I was feeling that I was giving in more than Jay was, but Jay was the head of our family and I trusted that he was doing his best for us. Unfortunately, I held onto these unvoiced, expectations of marriage. I could still see us, as old people, holding hands and walking down the beach together. That's how it was in the movies. Wasn't that how it was supposed to be?

When I mentioned that we worked together well, that included play. We were great tennis opponents, we loved water skiing, and we both loved to play softball. Jay actually sponsored a softball team for years during the summer and played with his friends. I played on a girls' team with my friends until Jay's team went co-ed. We both played pitcher/catcher so it was a natural that we would enjoy a supportive/offensive position with each other. We would constantly bicker which, most of the time, was actually quite fun! Of course, I was the better pitcher even though Jay could throw a back spin. This truth is not up for discussion at this time!

I played ball until our daughter decided she didn't want to be in the stroller any longer. Boy, I kept her there as long as I could because I knew it would be too difficult to play and watch her. Jay was too busy socializing to keep a good eye on her. Being a bit of a showman, Jay continued to have fun and get laughs, even though I wasn't the one egging him on. I'm big enough to admit that I was jealous at times, as I watched him teasing the other gals, because I was so insecure. Looking back, what a waste of effort that was . . . if I'd only known . . .

11

Back to life before child, I have to explain a few things. When we finally decided it was time for a family, it was discovered through testing and the process of elimination, that I had endometriosis which was causing infertility. It was one of those things that, if you didn't know that something was wrong, you thought it was normal. Some pain is just normal and I didn't realize the pain I was in, was abnormal. In short, I had two major surgeries and three minor ones to try to correct the problem. I was told there really is no cure besides menopause. I was in treatment for years. It was a very trying time for both of us, as well as a testament of our commitment to each other. Jay was a great source of support for me during my treatments. I know that my attitude was a bit jumpy at times and I spent a great deal of time recovering. Treatment included steroids for which I give the credit for hitting several home-runs that summer. Again, Jay was a good sport - life throws you curves.

During treatments and healing, our lives seemed to be on hold; sometimes you just go through the motions. As I mentioned, Jay worked on achieving Master Mechanic certification. I did whatever I could to help Jay in the shop. I did the accounting books for a while, did payroll, and helped work on cars after finishing my work day. Jay was able to employ a few part-time workers to help ease the load for himself. He also had a heart for the needy. A few times he even brought people home for the night, who needed a place to sleep. I admit, it was a bit scary at times, since I didn't know these people, but I trusted Jay's instincts. We lived in a small trailer park and didn't have much to steal anyway. I do believe a few of these people still keep in touch with Jay - evidence of Jay's good will.

12

My cousin used to throw Halloween parties every couple years. I mean big, awesome parties that had prizes for best costume and everything. They were adult parties. Our tradition at Halloween was usually to dress up our dogs (the kids) in costumes and trick-or-treat around the neighborhood. It was during this "in-between" time before child, that we attended our first party at my cousin's home. That year, it was actually held before Halloween and we went all out. Jay talked me into this idea of us going as a pimp and a hooker. However, our roles were to be reversed. Jay went to Goodwill and picked up a great dress for himself, a girdle, dress heels, wig, the works. He even wore water balloons in the bra. For me, I wore his mint green sport coat, an Afro wig and mustache, and put dark make-up on my face and hands. With my brown eyes, I knew there was no way to recognize me. I also "sold" watches under the sleeve of the sport coat. It was quite the get up and quite out of character for both of us.

It took the people at the party half an hour to realize that I wasn't a guy, another half hour to realize that Jay wasn't a woman, and another half hour to realize who we really were. It was loads of fun and we won the prize for best costumes. Since I was the designated driver, Jay had the time of his life. He truly enjoyed all the attention, and commented on how much fun it must be to be a hooker. He played it for all he was worth (personally, I thought he looked more like anybody's mom down at the polish bar – not that I'm judging). All in all, it was a successful night, but I couldn't dismiss Jay's comments about being a hooker. I was told to lighten up . . . it was just a party. Jay had to get under the hood of the car on the way home, to adjust something, and we giggled at the sight of him, arms up, dress over his hips, heels in the air . . .

However, when Halloween actually came, we again donned our costumes and made the rounds to our friends. I ate all the candy. Jay trick-or-treated with a glass. After visiting countless friends, we ended up at Jay's buddy's home. It seemed our host had also been drinking and when he brought out his pistols to show us, I really started getting disturbed. Jay ended up on his buddy's lap horsin' around and the water balloons broke. I don't think Jay even felt the cold water; they were all drunk and laughing so hard. It was not a very fun night for me. When I finally got Jay into the car so I could drive home, I was so furious, I could hardly think straight. I actually left him in the car, door open, throwing up and went into the trailer to go to bed. I didn't care what the neighbors thought. Hours later, I found him on the floor in the living room, half dressed, sound asleep. I covered him up and went back to bed. Of course, all was lost the next morning when Jay couldn't remember most of what happened. I confess that I hid those costumes down deep in the bottom of the closet and never expected to see them again.

13

Those years of surgeries and the unknown were not the best years. Stress puts elements of confusion and anger into normal life. Jay drank more after work. Every single month of finding out I was not pregnant, was a totally deflating moment for me. I'm not proud of myself as I know I caused many the argument over Jay's drinking and his actions. I was so disappointed in myself and my body, that I took it out on him. The commercial building where his auto shop was located, got sold. We moved his shop north to a pole building that needed some remodeling. It was our first venture in owning property and it was exactly what Jay was looking for. It should have serviced his needs for a very long time as it included room to grow. We again, combined our finances and talents to establish his new location. Since Jay was so handy with his hands, he did most of the remodeling work himself. I was able to help him with some of the heavy work that needed four hands. Unfortunately, when we tackled the heavy door slide above the garage door, Jay ended up with a torn thumb that required stitches. He was not normally a very patient person and he asked me to use some fingernail trimmers on the big flap of skin hanging off his thumb . . . I refused and took him to the hospital instead. He was always a bit accident prone. I borrowed money from my mom to buy a larger mobile home and we finally felt that we were moving into a more secure phase of our life.

I need to add a tidbit here about Jay being accident prone. During these years at the shop, he did odd jobs to fill in his time and need for cash. Some of these he did alone, and some he got friends to help with. One particular time, he was asked by a friend to help build a wooden seawall in front of his friend's house on the lake. Now, this friend also lived next door to my folks so I figured if I worked at my parents, I would be in close proximity if they needed any help. Since this friend was on the baseball team as well, these two guys together had a bit of a history of goofing off, so they asked me if it would be okay if they worked together. It required the use of a nail gun (they knew guns in general bothered me, so it was thoughtful that they asked). I jokingly said as long as they didn't shoot each other, it was fine.

There were always things to do at my parent's house so while the guys worked on the lake side, I was working across the street and could hear the hammering, noise, and laughter in the front yard. After a while, the guys came walking across the street to me, which I presumed meant they needed me to hold something. I giggled and said, "What happened, did someone get shot?" When the apologies started, it took me a minute to realize they were being serious . . . Jay had taken a nail in his chest! Apparently it had ricocheted off the original cement seawall and he had a bleeding hole next to his sternum right near his nipple. Well, he was standing and walking but starting to get pretty pale, so I asked my mom to call the hospital to warn them we were coming. We immediately put Jay in the car and started for the hospital twenty miles away (we had a Yugo at the time). I drove with Jay in the passenger seat. His buddy sat in the back but monitored Jay as there was not much room in a Yugo. There wasn't a lot of blood and you could feel the head of the nail close to the skin under Jay's arm; he was having no problem breathing so I didn't think it had hit his lung. Since I was worried about the possibility of shock, I put my emergency flashers on and hit eighty+ mph in that Yugo. Other drivers recognized my flashers as an emergency and moved out of the way for me, so we made pretty good time.

My mom had called the hospital but only told them that we were bringing in someone who had been shot. When we arrived, it looked like the whole hospital was out to greet us along with a few policemen. Obviously, when they heard "shot", they had another impression in their minds. Jay was in his glory! The doctors took x-rays to make sure the nail had missed everything important and they took pictures as they removed the nail. I guess it was a first time event for them as well. The neighbor (shooter!) remained by Jay's side and was profusely sorry. He was a good friend to my family and I forgave him for shooting my husband but we made it a pretty good joke for years. Ironically, this same man and his wife had fertility issues later in life. Jay was very helpful as he was experienced in giving shots to me, so he was part of their treatments at home. I know he felt pleased that he was able to give back and they remained good friends for years.

14

I was transferred into an infertility program which was an additional emotional strain on things. People came out of the woodwork with suggestions on how to get pregnant. I'm sure they all had good intentions at heart, but they didn't know how much we had already gone through, and didn't realize how much some of their comments hurt. They made it sound like they thought we were doing something wrong. Although I was told that I was in no way to blame for having endometriosis, I *felt* absolutely to blame why I couldn't conceive. Jay had also been "tested" and told that he had low sperm motility but the doctors did not feel it was the reason for my not getting pregnant. We were told that issues with men were usually easier to fix since the reproductive organs are easier to get to. This time of our life was an opportune occasion for Jay to have stood up and come forward with specific information about himself but he chose to keep quiet. We both kept our guilt *in* ourselves, *to* ourselves and tried to be strong for each other. We took comfort in our love for each other – hoping against hope that somehow things would work out.

Jay seemed to drink even more during these years of frustration. He would be out with his friends at night and come home drunk. One such night, after a binge, he broke down sobbing and started blubbering about himself. I sat on the floor, with Jay's head in my lap, trying to comfort him, and all I could make out was "nothing else matters except giving her a baby". It was as if he was trying to make a deal with God - if he could just give me a baby. Although I was mad about his drinking, I was equally curious about what he was talking about. Jay never admitted to any of this the next day and I finally just chalked it up to the collection of oddities in my mind.

Apparently, endometriosis is a genetic factor because all of the girls in my family (on both sides) seem to have fertility issues. It was during the time of my surgeries that we had some wonderful news. My sister was pregnant with her first child. The birth of my niece saved me from going crazy! On the other hand, the addition of a child can really shake up a relationship.

Being married is easy – staying married takes work. There are so many distractions in life that seem to pull couples apart that they forget about the long term benefits of staying married. In the past, families had to work together on the home, in the fields, with the children, in the church . . . it took the focus of two people looking together toward a common goal in order to reach it. The common goal of it all (to me) is to have someone beside you: to love, to fight with, to cry with, to cuddle with, to yell at - someone who loves you, someone who you can share your deepest thoughts and fears with, someone you trust, someone who trusts you. No one is perfect but hopefully, love wins out.

Life is a challenge. I think we all want someone we can trust to be there for us, at the end of the day, to come home to. Parents are examples for their children because that's how children learn best, by observing and watching. Parents can be good or bad but how they interact as adults, makes a difference in how their children view life. Since none of us are perfect, forgiveness needs to be a big factor in the love we show toward each other. Children learn love and forgiveness by watching the adults in their lives – not the adults on TV.

I was teaching horseback riding on the day my first niece was born. It seemed like such a long day before I could see her! She was the first grandchild as well and will always hold a special spot in my heart – she took some of the sting away from my own empty arms.

15

Originally, Jay and I had belonged to sister churches although we had not known each other. I had heard that he had dated every girl in church and he had heard, from one of his previous girlfriends, that I had dated every boy on the football team. Speaking for myself, I didn't even *know* anyone on the football team. After we wed, I played piano in both of our churches until another church was started in our home area. We participated in actually building the church and I continue to play piano there to this day. It is the people in this church that have stood by us the most. They were instrumental in prayers for my motherhood and continue with support and prayers for us in our day to day challenges.

We underwent invitro-fertilization (IVF) a total of three times. We encountered problems the first time through and had to add another medication the second time, in order to proceed again. The second time, the eggs were taken from me on the morning of Good Friday. Jay delivered his sperm in a jelly jar and the eggs were fertilized in a dish. They were then returned to me on Easter morning. The whole church, as a congregation, prayed for us that morning. The doctor joked about how the eggs weren't even "colored" like Easter eggs. I was told there were five out of eight that were viable - two super, two good, and an "iffy". He was kind of a strange man but he certainly knew his stuff. Two weeks later, I found out I was pregnant with one fetus. The third time we went through IVF, our daughter was two years old and I was told there was no point in any further treatment. God's answer was no more. We had been blessed with a daughter and my gift from God was the fact that I was a mom. I would need to turn in my heels for tennis shoes in order to keep up since life was about to change, again.

Anyone going through fertility issues, realizes that a lot of anxiety is placed upon the most personal, powerful, unpredictable, and spontaneous part of a marriage. You need to follow a specific timetable of intercourse which makes it a lot less fun. You need to chart temperatures, change work schedules, give yourself shots, or rely on someone else to give them to you, have blood drawn daily, take medications, just to give a few examples. I know that I was not the happiest camper through all of this, and I'm sure that Jay would admit to being a bear at times too. But he never voiced anger over it, and was always there to give me injections. Jay never seemed to doubt that it would work. When they gave the eggs back to me, I had to lay on my stomach for 4 hours . . . I *hate* to lay on my stomach! But Jay stayed right with me and read me a book and talked to me. He continued to attend church with me whenever he could and was very supportive to me, wanting to know all the details of pregnancy from my perspective. I mean, this was what we both really wanted so we both enjoyed the special time planning for our baby. I hoped the baby would bring us back together in another common goal. I was in 7th heaven.

It may have been the circumstances, or it may have been Jay's inner turmoil, but at a time when we should have been emotionally the closest, Jay started being physically driven. We had baby showers to attend and plans to make. My parents had given us some land as a wedding present and we decided it was time to move out of the trailer into our own house.

After much research, Jay decided he could build us a home. We moved the trailer to the vacant land, which was where Quaker had colic so many years before, and broke ground before our daughter was born. This home turned out to be the first home building project of Jay's new career. He bought a tractor that had a back hoe on one end, and a plow on the other. It was pretty old but Jay could fix up anything and he sure loved being on that tractor! I was on strict work restrictions so I was unable to lift much and it was SO HOT that summer. I remember that it was my job to put the "pins" in the cement forms as they were being put up for the basement. My sister was amazing as she replaced me as Jay's best worker. Our home was truly a family project because Jay's brothers put in many hours as well. In my mind's eye, I can still see Jay and his brother on the roof, all bundled up against the snow, trying to put a few more boards on. I say I still see them but at the time, I could hardly see them at all through the blowing snow. Because it was quite a ways off the road, we were blessed with a seclusion that made our property seem like a haven of sorts. It remains a bit unfinished to this day and I'm never really sure if I'm moving in or out. But it holds a lifetime of memories and I still call it home.

There are many happy memories of maternity for me. Jackie was pregnant as well and we attended Lamaze classes together. Her husband was a truck driver and not able to be home for the classes. Mine couldn't schedule the time to commit to the classes, so it worked out well for us girls. I was there when her son was born and it eased my mind thinking, if *she* could do it, *I* could do it. I was so proud of her! Unfortunately, after 36 hours of labor, our daughter was born by C-section. It actually was a blessing because I was allowed to stay at the hospital for five days and had the benefit of having nothing else to do but bond with my baby. Looking at it from this point in time, crazy as it sounds, I now find it a bit comforting that she was made in a Petri-dish.

16

"D" (daughter) was born on Sunday, December 17th at 1:02pm. I actually started contractions at 12:20am on Saturday. We had been to a company Christmas party, for my employer, Friday night and we'd had a great time eating and dancing. Although I didn't usually like to dance, I didn't seem to mind being a rather large, spectacle on the dance floor that night. Everyone was happy for us and we had a wonderful time. I loved being pregnant and I'd learned to laugh at myself more over the years. Jay had too much to drink so I drove home about 11:00pm. We got to bed about midnight. My contractions started five minutes apart at 12:20am. Since we'd been through IVF, the doctors pretty much knew when the baby would come and she was only 20 minutes late starting. I hung on through the night for several hours just to be sure it wasn't false labor and I knew that Jay needed to get some sleep. When I finally woke him, we grabbed the hospital bag and took off. It was snowing pretty hard when we got to the highway and we hoped we wouldn't have to turn around and return home right away. My contractions continued at five minutes apart for most of the day. We walked and walked around the hospital floor, trying to get some comfort from the activity and trying to speed things along.

At one point, the elevator doors opened and some carolers came off, singing beautiful Christmas songs. Unfortunately, I was in so much pain at that point, I almost pushed them back into the elevator!

We giggled about it later - it gave us a small distraction for a bit. I had been given a large private room and Jay slept on the couch as much as he could. It seemed like a super long day and both of our parents came later. I wasn't dilating as I should have been . . . probably because of my age for a first baby (I was thirty-four). Because I was exhausted due to lack of sleep, they gave me meds to ease some of the pain. Sometime in the night, they tried to induce labor and discovered that the baby had had a bowel movement which created a problem with waiting too long. I was prepped with an epidural and scheduled for surgery.

I remember surgery as being very cold. The tube from the epidural seemed like an ice river that traveled down my back. When they finally took the baby, I remember looking at her and shivering so badly that I was afraid to touch her. Her mass of hair and beautiful features were etched on my mind so that when she was wheeled past me, later in the day, I immediately recognized her. However, at the time of her birth, I declined to hold her and blissfully went to sleep. There are some great pictures of her having her first bath with her daddy and grandparents all around. It actually was a blessing that they were available to help at the perfect time. Jay was so proud of his daughter!

When I finally woke up a few hours later, I cleaned up and finally felt human. I walked down the hospital hallway looking for my baby. I'd already had a few surgeries on the same C-Section scar, so to me, the pain was minimal. Besides, the reward was so great! A few bassinettes were being wheeled by me in the hallway and I thought I recognized my baby. I stopped the nurse and asked if she was mine. After checking our ID's, she confirmed my parenthood and passed the baby over. Thus began my greatest adventure yet . . . I was a mom!

It seemed like everyone we knew came to the hospital to visit. That first afternoon was so busy, with everyone coming to congratulate us and hold the baby. I thought I was being generous passing her around but later, was told I had a hard time putting her down. My sister's family brought the cutest lamb toy that made a noise when you squeezed it. I still have it in storage for my daughter's future family. I've always said that "D" was a family project and the day of her birth proved that we had a big "family".

Having the Caesarean Section was truly a blessing because we could stay in the hospital longer, taking advantage of baby classes and being served my meals and learning how to transition into a parent. I so appreciated not having the responsibilities of all the animals at that time. I was bonding with my daughter and I cherish the memories of all the "first times" that I experienced in the hospital. I remember watching Jay with his daughter. He treated her with such gentleness . . . he was worried about his rough hands on her skin. Jay was beside himself with the joy of accomplishment. I knew that as soon as we got home, we'd have to find a new normal so we stopped time and enjoyed the arrival our daughter.

17

It was during the first year of our daughter's life, when another traumatic incident occurred. My sister and her husband were breaking up and she was in the phase of moving out of their home with her two girls. She lined up several people to help cart things out of the home, and we planned it for a day when her husband would be working . . . thus, ensuring no contact with him to make things uncomfortable. He knew they were moving out, but didn't know exactly when. Jay and I had left "D" with a baby-sitter and joined my parents and others at the farm site to help. My two small nieces were there to help pack their toys and clothes, and to make the move seem as normal as possible. Even my brother was there. Apparently, a neighbor called my brother-in-law at work and told him about activity at the house and he came roaring up in his car to create a nightmare.

Having been witness to some of the rage in my brother-in-law, I began to shudder when I heard the car pull in. I yelled up the stairs to my brother and heard him come bounding down the stairs to exit the home. Being the peace-maker, I followed my brother-in-law through the home trying to calm him down. I stopped talking as I watched him take down his rifle and load the gun with bullets. My mouth went dry as he pointed the gun directly at me and ordered me out of the house. I was horrified . . . this was something you saw on TV - it certainly wasn't something that happened in your own family! I joined the rest of the moving crew cowering in the yard.

It was a terrible confrontation as he accused us all of stealing and wrecking his marriage. His emotions were so raw, I don't know if he even knew what he was doing. He ranted and raved for what seemed like hours at the time, constantly aiming his rifle at us and swinging it around. There was a pregnant woman there, that I was afraid might have her baby on the spot. We all watched in horror as my husband became as unhinged as my brother-in-law. Jay got right into his face and started yelling back at him. He was saying things like, "Go ahead and shoot, I dare you!" This was a man that we had called family. I could not imagine what was going through Jay's mind in egging him on so. We all stood around like statues. My brother's face was white. Although he was aiming periodically at all of us, I knew that he hated Jay and my mom with a passion. My mind had already seen through to an end that I couldn't bear. I felt in my bones that it was not going to end well.

My sister's girls were watching wide-eyed at all of the activity, mercifully not understanding it. My car was filled with their toys, and I pleaded with their dad to let me take his children away. I reasoned that they didn't need to witness the things that were happening. He stopped his tirade long enough to check out my vehicle and gave permission for me to leave - no one else was allowed to go. I gathered the little girls, barefoot and scared, into my car and drove away. My last view of Jay, was of him pointing his finger in my brother-in-law's face, with three groups of other people huddled together, watching these men become unglued. I fully expected, as I drove away, that I would hear a gunshot.

By the time I loaded the kids into the car, we were all crying and I was trying to stay collected enough to drive. I made it down the road, listening all the way for gunfire and prayed with all my heart that God would keep them safe. I stopped at the convenience store down the road and asked them to call 911 to report the situation. I got the girls some ice cream while we were there and it successfully stopped their crying. The clerk was very kind. He made the phone call and served the girls even though they were barefoot. Apparently the authorities were already on their way to the house. Thank God for ice cream and small favors!

I turned the car around and drove back to the house, creeping along in case the police were not yet there and dreading what I might find. I didn't want the girls to see – they had finally stopped crying. There were no ambulances, which was a good sign, and things were definitely improved as I approached. People were milling about together and I could see my family still standing. The police had come and handcuffed my brother-in-law and discovered that the safety of the rifle had not been on.

We were very blessed that there were no injuries. However, I lived with a baseball bat next to my door for a year - mental injuries are so much worse because they play over, and over in your mind. I told myself I was protecting our daughter. Although my brother-in-law spent some time in jail, I couldn't shake my fear of him and guns. Also, I could not understand why Jay had to spur things on so. Didn't he care about his own family? Did he want to leave his daughter fatherless? I did not understand, at that time, how my husband felt about himself. Only much later was I able to piece things together and make sense of it in my own mind. I know that Jay was upset about how my sister's marriage was ending. Her husband was family, too. There was no more making excuses . . . Jay had simply reacted to the situation. Again, I can only write what I know from my side of the story, how things looked wearing my own shoes. My sister and the girls moved much closer to us which was a joy for me. My daughter and hers have created lasting ties which have allowed my daughter the semblance of sisters. Thank God for family! Love endures.

18

It was during this "middle" part of our marriage that my dad admitted himself to rehab for alcoholism. Although our entire family knew that dad drank a lot, none of us knew how much except mom. We had all seen his short temper and vague responses. We had watched as he came home late and had no time for family. My mom gave him an ultimatum and had somehow saved him from financially losing everything. I know he felt incredibly guilty about what he felt was his weakness. He tried to remain aloof when he returned from rehabilitation but we were so over-joyed to have him back, that we quickly forgave him for any backlashes suffered. We discovered a new "normal" as he came back to us a changed man. Sadly, he was left with health issues that stemmed from his drinking. They plagued him for the rest of his life. He picked up the pieces that were left of his business, and taught us about resilience. I especially loved his sense of humor. He discovered mail catalogs and took enjoyment in buying us the craziest things! Christmas was a hoot because you never knew if your gift from him was grand or goofy! My mom stood by him and showed us what true commitment was all about. She is one awesome lady.

Jay was unable to buy life insurance due to his racing hobby and eventually sold his race car (I think he was kicked off the track due to too many accidents). We were able to move the horses to our own property. "D" had the same benefit as I did, of living with nature all around us and grew up showing her pony and horse with the local 4H club. She was also on the high school equestrian team and I thanked God for her every day. She is a fantastic blend of both of us and has handled all of the challenges in our lives with grace. She has grown into a beautiful young lady with a compassionate heart toward others and is definitely her own person.

There are so many stories and memories involved with living and loving: times spent snowmobiling with family, boat parades and vacations. Our home was built more like a party house with high ceilings and a very large kitchen. We had many family gatherings, as well as pig roasts, that brought family and friends together. I cherish those times that are indelibly written in my mind because the emotion tied with them is real. It is only in the last few years that I can pull out pictures from the past and remember the happy family we were, instead of the damaged family that we had become. And we were happy - but there was a shadow across so much of it. Things that have happened more recently seem to have affected memories from the past. Jay was so busy with his business that he missed a lot of our family times. For many years, my folks brought us to Florida with them for spring vacations. They had a condo on the gulf side which was heaven! Jay missed quite a few of those trips due to business conflicts. I couldn't understand how business was more important than these wonderful opportunities with family, and I didn't understand the turmoil that was going on within him.

When "D" was five years old, Jay made special arrangements during spring break, to fly to Florida to be with my family for vacation. His dad was having heart surgery and Jay needed to know he was out of the woods before he would make the trip. Since the surgery went well, Jay arrived in Florida and spent a wonderful day at Disney with my folks and us. However, we were awoken in the night with a telegram stating that my father-in-law had passed away. Jay could not forgive himself for not being there. There were complications from a blood thinner that contributed in my father-in-law's death, but Jay was forever changed. Our vacation was cut short as we drove home to be with family. Jay and I sang a song together for the funeral. I agreed to sing to support my husband in his sorrow and also out of respect for the loss of a man I much admired and loved.

After the funeral, I could sense a withdrawal from family activities that had once been normal. There seemed to be no time for simple visiting anymore. He stayed away more with his friends and he partied harder; we lost the closeness of sharing that I longed for. Although I learned to value the benefits of the bedroom, I seldom initiated things and our Sunday ritual became more of an athletic event. Our friends actually kidded us about it being "Sunday" and had we done it yet? We laughed about it then, but I spent many a night crying by myself. Things were different but it was no use trying to talk to Jay about it, because the conversation was always one sided. He wouldn't talk about it. It was usually implied that I had done something to cause the problem anyway . . . whatever it was. Or at least, that is how it appeared to me. Besides, I had "D" which took up most of my time after work. The time I spent with her, helped ease my loneliness.

19

Jay used to complain that I stopped and smelled too many roses. Because I worked six days a week, for six months of the year, I cherished my time with "D". But I have to give credit where credit is due, because my family helped raise our daughter, too. When I worked on Saturdays, my mom and sister both fought over baby-sitting rights. If Jay was available, he would take over the position and "D" would tell me the grandest tales of where they went and what they did. I know that Jay loves her more than anything, but actions speak louder than words, and I felt that Jay should be spending more time with *us*. On the other hand, Jay felt I should be spending more time cleaning the house, among other things. Maybe he missed the time I used to put in at the shop. We were probably both right. Perhaps it was just the differences in our upbringing, but we each seemed to be listening to a different drummer.

When I had mentioned a change of career for Jay, he had decided that he really enjoyed building things. After he built our home, he sold his auto shop and started another business. He stated that he'd finally gotten tired of all the grease under his nails, so he taught himself the building trade, and started a construction company. He got a good start working on some of my dad's management projects. Jay's work crew did building maintenance projects and repairs when needed. I was also able to do some of these small jobs with Jay. When a job was scheduled for the weekends, Jay and I would usually be able to get the job done. Sometimes, it actually worked to our benefit since I was able to recycle some of the old lumber and supplies. There was always a need for an extra board or two at our place. I couldn't get quantity time with Jay but I could get quality time. I felt secure in the fact that we still worked well together and I liked the comradery that came from being a team.

Part of the major costs of building houses was having to order key components from others. Jay decided to branch out and built a small truss manufacturing plant in our pole barn in the side yard. His company could build the floor and roof trusses for the homes he built for others, thereby saving the cost of the middle man. He built the necessary frames and equipment to build the trusses himself. He obtained the CAD programs needed to design the trusses and taught himself how to use them. He was really good at it! Once the truss operations proved profitable, he started manufacturing trusses for other builders. We agreed that when the business made enough money, we'd move it to a larger, more permanent location. Jay was blessed with a proficient crew and a pretty good clientele. We were able to grow and obtained some heavy equipment that made the work easier. It actually worked out pretty sweet!

Of course, having the business right in my pole barn at home was both a godsend and a curse. It meant that Jay was home more, but it also meant that Jay was home more. It meant more people around and more traffic on our long, dirt-track driveway. It truly was a family business. "D" learned how to read a tape measure and had her own little tool belt. I stayed involved with the business as much as I was allowed to and learned how to read the angles necessary to cut the cross bars, press the plates on the trusses, and lend a hand with the heavy lifting. I actually got pretty good with a circular saw. Although I still did some payroll for Jay and we incorporated the business to protect our home, I was not involved as much with the books. Jay hired an accountant so I would have more free time. I was also drafted into helping erect some of those trusses which scared me half to death! Although Jay seemed fearless when faced with dangerous, physical challenges, he remained aloof in trying to work out the rift between us. A good example of how different we had grown, was in the fiasco of another Halloween party.

20

When "D" was about seven years old, she and I planned a Halloween party for a Saturday afternoon. Since our home was at the end of an 1800 foot, cross country driveway, we were a bit secluded and didn't have many friends outside of business, and no real neighbors. We had purchased party favors, planned games, sent out invitations and were looking forward to some fun with family and some friends from school. Jay planned on working in the shop with a few employees, during the afternoon party. At that time, I had been working in the public school system as a paraprofessional for a few years, and was excited to meet some of the parents of our daughter's school mates.

I'm still not sure why, but my husband decided to have an impromptu party of his own that same late afternoon, without mentioning a word of it to me. The kids arrived and some parents stayed to help with the party and enjoy the fun. We bobbed for apples, had broomstick races around the circle drive, and had a joyous time. After the games, my husband started a bonfire which was in the middle of our "race track" and his crew showed up. He didn't have many workers then but the ones he had, stayed to party. Some wives and girlfriends showed up as well. They started out drinking a few beers around the campfire while we finished up with our party. I had some funny Halloween music from the Muppets, playing outside most of the afternoon but Jay switched that to a truly scary CD that sent the rest of our guests scurrying for home. "D" and

I watched from the window as Jays friends came and went that night. We heard them singing (Jay took out his guitar), drinking and joking around. Although they were all very nice people, their language got out of control when they were drinking. They all looked like they were enjoying themselves and no one seemed to be missing me . . . it caused a bigger gap between us. "D" doesn't like Halloween to this day, even though she says she doesn't remember most of that night, except the music.

Interestingly, those costumes I had hidden years ago, the ones from the pimp and hooker party, I found them again while looking for Halloween decorations and other costumes. I almost pushed them aside to see what else was in the back of the closet, but something caught my eye and demanded a closer look. The wig looked pretty ratty - I even wondered, vaguely, if a mouse had gotten into it. And the high heel shoes my husband had worn (size eleven) looked pretty old and ragged. In the back of my mind, I kind of wondered if my nieces had been playing with them, as I remembered them as being in much better shape. The girls had outgrown my size seven's and would naturally have played with these had they found them. Thinking no more about it, I tossed them in the back, continued digging and eventually found what I was looking for.

Apparently, there were things happening outside of our immediate family as well. To this day, I do not know what went on between my sister and my husband, but they spent a lot of time not talking to each other – I mean *years*. Family get-togethers were becoming a horrendous ordeal that Jay chose to ignore. Neither one of them would discuss it with me. As it was, I couldn't successfully explain to "D" why daddy could miss the party, but she couldn't. I hate double standards.

21

Working for the school system meant that I had days off when the students had days off. I am a para-pro so, although I don't make as much money as a teacher, I am home when my daughter is home. To me, that's worth its weight in gold! After Thanksgiving (1997), we used the next day to catch up on things. Jay poked around in the pole barn amongst the sawdust and forms. It was a quiet day that I remember: enjoying leftovers from our Thanksgiving meal, a simple day together.

Shortly after midnight, we were awoken by a pounding on the front door. When we opened our eyes, it was apparent that we had no power and a strange glow showed through the windows. As I opened the bedroom door, to get to the front of the house, I could see through the windows that there were mountains of flames coming from the pole barn! I started screaming for Jay to get "D" and proceeded to answer the knocking at the front door. I met a fireman, who said we had to leave RIGHT NOW. As Jay brought our daughter from her bedroom, I grabbed her winter coat to put on her over her pajamas and threw a snowmobile outfit over mine. We gathered the dogs and started out of the house as explosions lit the night air. The truss work crew used spray cans of paint to mark the ends of the trusses, and the stored cans were the cause of all the explosions. Jay had built our home with 2X6" walls, and the fire had started in the pole barn which was at the opposite end of the house from our bedrooms. We had slept through booms that had woken the neighbors a mile away!

As we were escorted by the fireman, away from the flames of the pole barn, fire trucks were making their way up the snowy, quarter mile driveway. It turns out that, while on another call, that fireman had actually been close enough to see the fire and ran through woods, deep snow, horse pastures and barbed-wire fences, in the dark, to knock on our front door and probably saved our lives. I remain so very grateful to that man! Reports later stated that ours was the only house actually saved that year. The actual cause of the fire was never determined. In any case, it was an accident. Buildings can be replaced. People can't.

I know in my heart, one good thing that came from the fire, was that Jay and my sister came to terms with each other. My sister lives at the end of our drive and was positively out of her mind with worry, as more and more emergency vehicles passed her house. She ran all the way up our driveway, dodging fire trucks, firemen, and onlookers that showed up, until she found us. The vision of her and Jay hugging, tears streaming down their faces, with flames dancing into view behind them, is burned into my memory. Jay stayed with the firemen, running around in frustration, while we walked past my sister's home and camped out at my mom and dad's house further down the street. They were actually snowmobiling up north that weekend so, knowing they would not have heard about it, we waited until dawn to call them and let them know the extent of the damage. No one was injured, the animals were safe and sound. The side of the house was pretty well melted, with windows broken, but it could have been so much worse. However, the pole barn and business was a complete loss and I remember how it looked: like a horrible, broken, twisted, carnival ride. People laugh at me now when I am so overly careful with bonfires, but I remember the extreme fear and feeling of helplessness that resulted from that fire. I watch a burning bonfire until the bitter end. Better safe than sorry - always!

I wish I could say that life was better after that. Jay and I had to work together to put our lives back in order for "D". Her playhouse had burned so Jay made sure it was fixed first, hoping it would ease some of the frightening memories of that night. Some things improved but other things didn't. I guess the only thing you can count on in life, is that things will change.

My duties at the school were very satisfying for me. I loved my job with the kids, and I continued to teach HRH on Saturdays. I have to add that family and friends were indescribably generous in their support of us during this time. Cards and calls kept coming with words of encouragement or money to help us out. My friend, Marie, had been through a fire in her lifetime. She was extremely helpful in clean up and on how to protect the carpets, since ash was everywhere outside. With heavy snow on the ground, as well as the debris and soot, it was more than a mess.

With the loss of the business, and our livelihood, Jay had some choices to make. Of course, the pole barn was under-insured and Jay spent many days hashing things out with the insurance company. When we got a go-ahead from the township, we purchased a building permit and started rebuilding the pole barn with intentions of making it better than it was. Jay organized a barn raising weekend with family and friends, and the work began. The basic structure went up almost overnight. However, a week into the work, the township rescinded the building permit and tied it all up in court. They decided they did not want any business back there and they would not make any concessions or compromises.

Apparently, Jay had not made many friends around our immediate area and he didn't get any support from our rather distant neighbors. They really did not want to help us out at all, so in order to rebuild the pole barn, we had to agree to not ever have any sort of business on our ten acres. There was someone from the township who actually took pictures of us rebuilding the pole barn, from a point on our own property, which was illegal. Talk about above the law?! The legality of this evidence resulted in only a slap on the wrist for the photographer, since we were not doing any wrongdoing. Regardless, we had no choice as we could not afford the time or money to battle their decision in court. Therefore, Jay took out a second mortgage on our home and we relocated the business again. The payment of this mortgage came out of Jay's earnings since the money went to relocating the shop.

Jay found property only eleven minutes away from our home which, again, seemed like the ideal place for his business. It had an office and a very large pole building which he converted into his truss manufacturing plant. Over the next couple of years, he worked his tail off, trying to do and be everything that was necessary for the business. His workers moved with him to this new location - he had some very committed people and good friends. Perhaps they couldn't say "no" either?! I knew my husband could do anything he put his mind to.

Once the business was moved, life returned to a more normal routine at home. Jay was gone most of the time. Our daughter was older and finding it more of a chore to go with dad, although she learned quite a bit from him as well. There were a lot of educational and financial changes to the school systems. Although I was fortunate to be able to work for community education during the summer months, every fall meant the worry of whether or not I would have placement within the school system. Hours were taken away from all para-pros and wages were decreased. That worry continues to this day and has become an occupational hazard that takes its toll.

22

I am not sure of when, but on his own, Jay approached my dad for additional funding for the new location. We had always planned to move the business, but had hoped it would be under more prosperous circumstances. Over the years, Jay had proven himself to be a shrewd business man and my dad believed that Jay could put his money where his mouth was, so to speak. Remember, Jay was a hard person to say no to?! I believe that my dad loved Jay as a son and wanted to see us succeed.

With more working capital, the business started to regain a good clientele. It seemed that Jay found ways to take it easy a bit during the days and not, personally, have to work so hard. He trusted his work crew that much. In fact, I found out that Jay would actually travel over 75 miles away to get his hair cut by a particular person! I was in shock over that one . . . he also started wearing some rather interesting fashions. Being of a shorter height, apparently clothes that fit comfortably were harder to find. I know that I shortened my fair share of pants for him, but I couldn't really understand the girl's cutoffs. Jay said that they fit better and were cheaper. Why should I care?! Anyway, I guess I chose to not make a hassle over such a minor detail as work clothes. And I loved saving a buck!

My folks wanted the entire family to travel to Florida with them to celebrate the upcoming Y2K New Year. My dad was undergoing kidney dialysis at the time, and we were all hoping this would be a very special time with family. This involved my sister's and brother's families as well. After much pleading and consideration, Jay agreed to go. My folks drove their motor home down thereby taking their time - they actually stayed there longer and besides, we'd have a vehicle down there then as well. Dad was having dialysis at night so having the medical equipment right on board the motor home, helped save on down time. My folks supplied the condos, we supplied the fun!

The airplane trip was a riot! There were eleven of us and we all had to actually run from runway to runway, trying to catch all the transfers. We had a great time getting reacquainted with each other. It was seldom that we all had real, valuable time to spend with each other. Although we all lived close to each other, our busy lives didn't cross very often – basically, Christmas was the family gathering time. The weather that December, was cold and rainy but there was plenty of warmth inside. We swam in the pool (in the rain) and played monopoly for hours upon hours. We rode bikes and went out to eat at fun restaurants. I distinctly remember getting caught under an awning with my mom and "D", while riding bikes in the rain. The kids had a blast - so did we! I don't think I've laughed as hard since.

Although the weather was chilly, we all got as much sun as possible and enjoyed the beach on the gulf. When it is 10° at home, 60° feels great! Although it was a bit chilly, I couldn't help but notice that Jay never took his shirt off. He even swam in the pool and fished on the beach in his t-shirt. It seemed quite natural at the time because it was so cold, but it was out of character for him. He loved to fish so we had fun visiting the fishing piers that we knew from the past. I relish the memories of that trip since it was our last one spent together. Since the weather was so poor, we didn't take many pictures but we were able to capture an entire family portrait at the condo. If I'd known it was the last time we'd all be together like that, I would have taken more pictures and paid more attention.

23

Sadly, our relationship continued its slow, downward spiral. There was very little personal communication between us. "D" was having some health issues that worried us, so she was our biggest concern. Jay had found a band that he really admired and spent many a night at the bar listening. I even hired them to come to our house and play for his birthday party! Boy, were they good. Jay became one of their roadies when they traveled, and he started leaving his workers in charge at the shop more often. I continued to be involved when needed. I'd type up the invoices and sometimes help out in the shop, building the trusses. It seemed the only way I could be involved with Jay at all, was to work with him. Unfortunately, I began to see a change in his work ethics and I was losing respect for some of the ways he handled business. Jay seemed to be more introverted and less patient with people. He'd stopped pretending he liked anyone at church; he refused to come to family visits. If I truly insisted, he would make an appearance and be very uncooperative doing it which, of course, made everyone else uncomfortable as well.

It was like we started living separate lives. It seemed the only thing keeping us together was our daughter. I know he loved her dearly. The sad part was, I knew he loved *me*, but I wasn't sure what had happened that he didn't *like* me anymore. When Jay, as a roadie, followed his band down to Key West, I don't think he intended on making it home. He called from several points on the east coast, and said he thought he'd drive through New York City before coming home. I listened, and quietly said I thought he should come home *now*. I think I instinctively knew that I wouldn't see him again, if he didn't come then. Somehow, reason won out and Jay physically arrived but he never really came home. He spoke of fun nights and drinking. It seems the band even wrote a song about him. I listened.

Since I worked with children, I had kicked the nicer dress clothes in favor of comfort. I was more comfortable in my own fashions and found it much easier to play and work with students, if I wasn't worried about my clothes. Looking back on it now, I realize that I may also have been trying to make myself look less desirable. I was not as eager to attract sexual attention to myself, especially from my husband. In retrospect, I wonder if my outward appearance was simply a reflection of my own inner turmoil?! In some ways, I know I was shutting down or maybe, just shutting off.

Sometime in March 2001, I wasn't paying that much attention to it, my husband and I had our last romp in bed. It had been months since we'd even hugged each other, and I couldn't help but notice that his body had changed. As I touched his chest, I noticed that both of his breasts had small, hard lumps on them. I was very concerned, to the point that activity stopped. Upon questioning him, his comment was simply that it was okay, it would go away with time. But it wasn't okay and I knew there were things that Jay wasn't telling me. Distrust raised its ugly head in my mind. The fun that morning was done.

Later that month, my daughter and I made our usual plans for vacationing in Florida during Spring Break with my folks. Jay voiced that he had no interest in coming with us, although he gave his regrets. My dad's declining health continued to be a big concern, and we balanced our time between enjoying the wonderful surroundings and spending precious time with my folks. We have been so blessed over the years, to share in this wonderful place with my parents and family. I have had the chance to see love in action first hand. I've watched as my folks supported each other in finances, health, pain, financial ruin, and even in death. But mostly in love . . .

The summer of 2001 was busy. I hardly even noticed the fact

that Jay was not around much, but I must say, he always came home. He was sporting a different, longer hair style and I noticed a distinct shine to his nails that he attributed to chemicals at work. I could not bring myself to interact in bed anymore (I could feel myself drawing away when he hugged me), but I always knew when he came home and crawled into bed. I found comfort in that. Our daughter was eleven years old and facing some major changes in her own life. I felt there was a good chance of life going on like this forever and I was not happy. I think I just gave up trying to figure it out and accepted life day by day.

I remembered all the good times, and difficult times, that we had struggled through together. It's funny how the brain sees things in retrospect. Jay and I had shared so much in our lives together, that I just couldn't let go. I was willing to accept whatever Jay could give me and I kept praying for more.

However, I could not find my husband to reason with - and he did not want to be found. When I tried to confront him, we would inevitably have a fight. The last time I tried, I cornered him in the bathroom, thinking he was a captive audience. Jay put his fists through the wall of our bathroom . . . one on either side of my head. Somehow I knew, as his fists were coming at me, that he wouldn't really hit me. Needless to say, our argument was immediately over. Jay made a doorway where the holes were, and divided the bathroom into two. He turned it into a master bathroom which made another door that could be shut between us.

24

On Sunday, August 19th, 2001, around 4:00am, I rolled over in bed and put my arm around Jay. Presuming he was sleeping, I snuggled a bit and mumbled, "We can't go on like this". We had an end-of-summer party scheduled that weekend at my parent's house with my mom's side of the family. I just couldn't sleep as I was worried about the party. To my surprise, Jay was awake and had heard my mumbled words. He broke down in tears and started talking about his "secret". I had to keep my arm steady across his shoulders, as his words began to sink in and my world started to crumble.

As more and more words came spewing out of his mouth, more and more things started to surface in my mind. I must have been holding my breath because I remember starting to tremble as I held onto him. As my mind was trying to grasp the things he was saying, a small bell seemed to be going off in my brain. It seemed like the other shoe was finally making an appearance . . . and it was not even from the same pair of shoes. Our life would never be the same again. It was absolutely devastating!

Apparently, Jay had known he was different from an early age. When young children interact, they quickly learn from other people's reactions, what is acceptable and what is not. And kids can be cruel. Jay learned to go along with the crowd rather than be singled out as different. As Jay talked that morning, my mind was abruptly waking up.

At first, I thought Jay was going to admit to having an affair. I half expected that. But then I thought that he was telling me he was gay. That, in itself, would not be the end of the world. As the pent up emotions and words kept coming, it finally hit my befuddled brain that the man I married, was telling me he was a woman. While my arms held my sobbing husband, my heart plummeted to the floor where it was shattered beneath the other shoe.

While part of my mind was actively listening to the almost incoherent confessions of my husband, the other part of my mind wandered through our life together, reliving certain times that had baffled me. I tried so hard not to move a muscle, fearing that any movement would seem to be judgmental to my husband, and he would clam up. In retrospect, I don't think he could have stopped if he had wanted to.

As he told me of his "journey" through life, peering through his confused eyes, I inwardly cringed at the tales of horror. I tried to put myself in his shoes, in order to understand his life of, what sounded like, prison. In short, when he looked into a mirror, he never saw the person that he felt he was. He had to outwardly conform to the person that the world said he was, instead of experiencing the life that his own mind told him should be his. The world had called him male. He knew he was female.

We stayed in bed and talked for hours until "D" finally found her way into our room. My head was spinning with questions for Jay and with fear of the unknown to come. I could feel my heart starting to shrink and wither . . . I had a physical pain in my chest! We agreed that for today, we would say nothing to anyone about this grave admission and crossroads in our lives. I use the word crossroads because, in my mind at least, there was a glimmer of hope . . . hope for me because I had thought for all these many years, that there was something wrong with *me*. It was a crossroads for Jay because, intuitively, I knew that this knowledge would forever change the way we lived and loved. I began the mourning process for our life and my partner.

I don't remember much about that weekend. It seemed as though

I was looking through everything in slow motion. I must have played piano for church - that was the usual norm for Sundays. I remember watching my relatives talk to me at the party that afternoon, but I couldn't tell you a word that they said. My mom, bless her heart, knew something was wrong but she held her peace for the day. The family enjoyed the water and boat rides – it's usually a full, fun day when we all get together. It should have been a day to cherish, since it was the last social gathering my husband went to with my family. However, we were so wrapped up in trying to act normal, that I lost the whole day just trying to hold it all together. One thing was very clear about our morning revelations. Things were about to change drastically and I needed to make sure that our daughter was emotionally protected from the brunt of it.

25

Apparently, Jay had been seeing a "counselor" for some time regarding this conflict in his life. I mean for *years*. Jay begged me to go with him to see her immediately. For the sake of our family, I agreed. He set up an appointment two days away and, since school hadn't started yet, I asked my mom to watch "D" while we were gone. Knowing something big was in the wind, Mom agreed to watch her and agreed not to question me for a few days. Interestingly, this therapist was very close to the area where Jay would go to get his hair cut. It seemed as though the puzzle pieces were finally beginning to fit together. It seemed, too, that my parents were holding their own piece to the puzzle, which I didn't find out about until much later.

With school not in session, I had the week off as well, so timing was great – God's work in progress. I had a day to gather my thoughts before we would see this professional. I spent that day at my mom's, helping her do some cleaning and yardwork. True to her word, she did not hound me about the situation and the longer the day got, the madder I became. It was very hard not to confide in Mom, but I knew that this was a matter between Jay and me first. As I climbed the ladder to wash her windows, I could feel the tension entering my body. Memories from the past, of our life together, kept popping into my head. Although I could put myself in Jay's place, and understand a bit of what he went through, I was beginning to remember how absent he had been in our lives and I was an emotional basket case by the end of the day. I'm ashamed to say that I was also feeling quite used.

Although the appointment was only a couple hours away, it seemed to take forever to get there. We had to stop along the way, in order to get through the emotional challenges of the trip. It was difficult for Jay to drive through the emotional tears . . . we spoke of past "trips" and we both cried most of the way there. I had this pit in the bottom of my stomach that was not going to go away for a long time. We talked all the way there - somehow trying to release the pain of losing the world we knew. We cried for the past, and for the future. We had to face the present.

As soon as Jay started talking about being trapped in the wrong body, my mind took me back to some college classes I had taken. My science professor had included various abnormalities in humans and animals in his case studies. I also recalled my psychology professor having a few chapters on identity and the influence of our own psyche on our inner most being. I instinctively knew that my husband had been hounded by devils in his life, but I had no idea it was so all encompassing. I think, at first, I was just trying to find ways to make this go away . . . to stop it from going any further down this irreversible path. It hurt too much!

Working with impaired individuals in the HRH program has taught me to have empathy towards others. I was also working within the school district in the special services category. I'd been exposed to many abnormal situations and circumstances (although none with identity issues), so I sped toward this meeting with the last dredges of hope. I wanted it all to be a nightmare – I wanted to wake up! My mind careens away from putting myself back in that place and time. I admit, I must have been in shock because at that time, I could only cry and listen to everything that was said. I was told of the history of my husband's gender crisis. At least, of what was believed to be the reason for my husband's circumstance. I was given medical reasons that may have occurred while Jay was still developing in the womb. I learned that he was considered transgendered. He had gone through life hiding the fact that he wanted to have been, and felt he should have been, the one in the prom dress. He felt resentful of girls that had so much fun with their hair, and clothes, and shoes (remember that one!), and dates. Apparently, Jay had hoped that our marriage would make his other needs less intense. He had hoped that by being a "father", he could quiet that other voice in his head that said, "But what about *me*?" Having suppressed so many emotions all of his life, Jay was left with depression - enough so that he had even considered suicide several times. Remember the late nights and not wanting to come back from Key West?

Jay had found this counselor out of sheer desperation and the counselor had been advising him during this transitional stage for years. Apparently, Jay had decided that his only recourse was to have the necessary surgery to become a woman. I was told that he had made this decision months ago and could not be swayed from it. The hardening in his nipples had been from the hormones that he had already started taking. He'd made this decision without any thought of asking me . . . he had managed to tell others in his life, including his work crew, but couldn't tell his life's companion. They had also found a possible way to financially help Jay accomplish this major, reassignment surgery. The hardship was, he had to successfully live as a woman for a year before they would do the surgery. I was encouraged to support my husband, whom I loved and who still loved me, and I felt quite cornered. It seemed that they had it all worked out!

I was absolutely broken. Although this information illuminated so many things from the past, I could not believe that Jay hadn't trusted me with the truth. After all, with everything we had been through with infertility alone, I couldn't believe he had kept this from me. After 24 years of marriage, Jay had made the decision to go on hormones by himself. His comments during our last sexual exchange finally made sense. He was preparing for a life as a woman and he said he needed my help?!

When I first understood what Jay was talking about, my internal self was flashing back over the course of our lives together. As Jay spoke about his own past and our life together, my mind was reliving those same times. Our life had certainly been full of conflict, but there were such wonderful times as well. Our time together out of state, when we first got married, where we had to rely on each other for everything, was precious to me. Living in the close confines of a motor home for 6 months forced us to build a close companionship. We shared dreams . . . he had wanted his own garage and I had wanted a home and family. We played badminton, went to auctions, spent time actually learning about each other, or so I thought. Walking sick horses and watching our new baby sleep, I thought our relationship was based on trust. As Jay related the same stories from the past, from his point of view, I was feeling betrayed and confused.

The other part of my mind, the practical side, was also speeding along on another highway. I call this my "God led" side because it was going to teach me to talk, if not for myself, then for our daughter. My immediate concern was for protecting her from the onslaught of misinformed, misguided people and their opinion of gender issues. It was not a time in society for acceptance of anything outside of the "norm" and for most people in my circle of life, this was definitely outside of the norm. Although I had to accept this decision that my husband made, for himself, I could not accept it within our marriage. I knew that our marriage was over but I actually had known it back in March, when I realized he was lying to me. Now, I finally knew why. My heart was telling me that I had to support my husband in his decision, before any ties could be cut. As far as our marriage was concerned, I believed that the future would somehow take care of itself.

Both the counselor and Jay were telling me that life didn't have to change immediately. They brought several different scenarios to my attention, which convinced me that this conference had been going on much longer than I was first led to believe. It seemed that Jay had been having electrolysis treatments, as well as group therapy sessions, for quite some time. No wonder he was seldom home! No wonder we never had any extra money! They even tried to convince me that there was no reason that sex couldn't continue until the surgery was done. I declined, knowing that if my husband thought he was a woman, I could not have sex with a woman. I'm ashamed to say that I had a hard time even hugging him since our last encounter – the emotional pain was already starting. In fact, I kind of joked later that had I known, in March, that it would be the last time we were together, maybe I would have paid more attention . . .

I had not been able to even think about getting together sexually with Jay since March. I guess we are truly slaves to our hormones because knowing now, that Jay had been on hormones then, made it perfectly clear that my body knew more than I did. Sadly, I had shied away from even a hug from him. Now, I tried to accept him as the woman he said he was and tried to hide my pain from others and him. It would do no good now. Apparently, there was an organization that wanted to do a documentary on the subject of gender changes and they were looking at Jay's case study. The crux was that they needed to be able to interview both sides; they needed to be able to present the pros and cons of the issues from both sides of the marriage and from both sides of the gender issue. They already had a couple to film, regarding the change of female to male. They wanted me to be part of this interview process - to open up our lives to a film crew, and to let them into our home and personal feelings. In return for this intrusion, they would help defray the extreme cost of the surgery for Jay. This documentary was particularly important to Jay because he thought it would be beneficial to anyone else born with this "condition". He liked the thought of helping others. I was appalled at the whole idea . . . I had lots to think about.

I don't even remember the ride home from the counselor. My mind was spinning in an effort to take it all in. A parallel view of the world was opening up to me and I was terrified of what was down there. I had decided not to act hastily, to try to keep the damage under control as much as possible, because we were talking of our family, our business, our income, our social standings, and our future.

26

It was apparent that Jay was much more focused on the ending "pages", and had already done some research on informing his customers of the changes forthcoming in his life. Lots of reading material suddenly appeared regarding transgendered families and making things "work". There were children's books about blended families and how to relate to adoptions for transgendered parents. I'm sure that very educated people wrote those books. but they were no comfort to me. I was told that in order for a patient to undergo re-assignment surgery, you have to have successfully lived as the "opposite sex" for a full year. The word successfully here, means that the transgendered person needs to be accepted and adapted to his/her new life. This massive change to our relationship would be taking at least a year to complete. The ending chapter for my husband, would be a "new woman". My reward was a year of watching my husband (and "D's" daddy) die. I still could not say no to the person I loved and had married. I was still confused as to my own devotion to "in sickness and in health". As an act of symbolism, I put my wedding ring on the other hand.

The most important thing, in my mind, was how it would affect our daughter. I was "told" by Jay and his adviser that I needed to be "open-minded" about it. Well, I must say that I felt I was being VERY open-minded, but that didn't mean that I had to agree with it all. Jay made the decision on his own to start on hormones, and had planned to just "go away" before that fateful morning when I finally learned about Jay's condition. I believe this was all God's timing because I have no idea when Jay would have left or if he would have confided in me beforehand.

From the information I remember from my college days, as well as from the information I have gleaned over the years working with impaired individuals, I truly believe transgenderism is a birth defect. I also couldn't kick him when he was down, so, I dutifully began calling Jay "she", and the new name she had picked out was Jae. I have chosen not to use Jay/Jae's real name as to protect her from any unwanted notoriety. It is also to separate my story from hers - she has told her own story in the documentary. Although I had decided to support Jae in her endeavor to find herself, I wasn't fooling myself into thinking life would go on as it had. I knew in my heart, that my marriage was over and I took whatever comfort I could, from realizing that it wasn't all my fault. We all carry baggage with us: memories of bad choices, things we'd rather forget. I tend to be a bit paranoid because of all the emotions I have ignored within myself. Many people advised me against supporting my husband through all of this, but I was committed to my husband as long as he needed me. It may sound stupid but in sickness and in health . . .

After deciding on her course of action, our immediate plan was to tell our daughter and families respectfully. Jae had a time limit set for herself and she didn't seem to see the difficulty in that for me. She wanted to begin her year as soon as possible, since there were people involved in Jae's life that knew already. I'm sure that word was already out on some levels. On the other hand, I had a really hard time dealing with that because I felt betrayed. Some of these people were business associates and some were "friends". At least, I had thought they were my friends as well, but the longer we went into this transition, the blinders came off and the angrier I got.

My parents were very confused and feeling a bit guilty. They had received a phone call a few weeks before all of this, from a mutual friend, that said they had seen Jay walking on a sidewalk in a neighboring city, dressed like a woman. My folks had laughed about it and didn't believe it, so they had not shared it with me. Now, they really felt guilty in not responding to this information. I knew there was nothing that would have changed because I would have laughed about it, too. In retrospect, all the crazy things that were "Jay", were finally coming into focus. Well, so I thought.

We spent the next day with our daughter and tried to find the words to explain what was going to happen. Not the surgery part of course, but the fact that "daddy" was going to start dressing like a girl. I'm not sure if anything we said was going to make much sense to an eleven year old girl, but she listened to Jae's explanation and didn't question it. "D" was going into 5th grade and admittedly, spent most of her time between her friends and the 4H club. Although she avoided being seen with her dad, to my knowledge, she never voiced negative words about it. I am SO proud of our daughter! I continue to learn from her to this day. Her acceptance of her "dad" was not total but she knew that "daddy" loved her. I talked to the parents of her closest friends (three families), and tried to explain the situation. At times, I was a complete train wreck and was unsure of what to do. These amazing folks were tolerant and were able to give our daughter, and me, verbal reassurance and hugs when we needed it.

This "news" was leaking fast so we took the remainder of the week and spoke to the rest of our families. My mom, bless her heart, has never said "I told you so" and she has stood by me to the bitter end. Dad was beginning to have worsening health issues and I blamed myself for more stress in his life. He said just the opposite; he said that I was keeping him alive.

That was such a painful week. I received much comfort from my family at that time. One cousin's first comment, about hearing of Jae's challenges was, "Of course he is . . . that answers everything!" My old school friends continued to stand by me, although their husbands were not as forgiving. Some of these people were old drinking buddies; some were friends from the ball team. These had been Jay's guy friends and I realize that guys talk about different things than girls. They poured their guts out to each other over every pitcher of beer they drank, and they distrusted this new person they thought they had known. I know how they felt. I know there were a LOT of people who had a hard time accepting Jay as Jae - I could not blame anyone if they chose not to stand by us during this "change". People have to make their own choices. My husband was gone and all I could do was help pave a life for Jae. The time table of our life was revolving around Jae.

Up to that point, I think that was the most trying week of my life and by Saturday, I was in the hospital with kidney stones. "D" and I were on a pre-planned shopping trip (therapy!) and I had to stop into the hospital on the way, due to the pain in my side. I kept saying, "I'm under a lot of stress . . .", but they kept saying stress had nothing to do with it. I beg to differ. Apparently vitamin C and caffeine (Coca-Cola) don't mix, so at least I learned something as I take a lot of vitamin C daily. We were there all day waiting for me to pass the stones and waiting for Jae to come pick us up. "D" spent that time playing with whatever she could find in my purse, listening to me moan. I'd had so many pain medicines, they wouldn't let me drive home. We were there for about ten hours, waiting for Jae because she was at an out of town meeting with her "peers". I felt the first pangs of embarrassment when Jae came in to sign me out. The hospital staff knew I was waiting for my husband and when Jae walked in, I could see the surprise in their faces. I imagine that "D" felt the same way but she admits that she has blocked a lot of years from her memory and won't talk about it. I had thought I was someone who didn't care what the world thought. I guess I was wrong about that. I did care and I was ashamed that I was so shallow.

My encounter with kidney stones was on August 25th and on September 11th, our country came under attack. It was during these two weeks that I found out that I was laid off from the school system (God was still at work). I had some time at home to re-coup my health and my emotions. For some reason, 4:00am became Jae's and my unscheduled conference time. We never planned it, but it seemed that we were both awake and we'd take advantage of the fact that "D" was sleeping. We could plan, reminisce, cry and just whisper in peace. I was accepting the fact that Jae had to get some things out in the open and off her chest; there was no need for me to comment during most of these conversations. There were some things she related, that I saw completely different but knew that I needed to wait until the time was right for me to comment. Jae continued to say that we were still the same people and since she hadn't "changed" yet, we could still carry on sexually . . . we were married. I unconditionally declined but carried my own burden of desire for the man that I married. I felt very much alone.

27

When I admitted that I carried some scars from these years and events, I was not exaggerating. Since I was the "quiet" type anyway, my mind was playing tricks on me. For example, when I got called back in to work, at a different school within the district, I imagined that everyone knew, was looking at me and somehow judging me. I admit, I was being paranoid but sexual identity is something so personal. In my mind, I was feeling that my own self-image was under attack. "D" was in a new school in the fall, and Jae and I approached the teachers with the news that her parents were different. It was pretty obvious that the teachers were a bit uncomfortable with the conversation, but to be fair, they took it in stride and never spoke of it in front of "D" at school. The school psychologist took "D" under her wing and would leave little gifts in her locker; she always had a smile or quick hug for her to let her know she was thinking of her. Although "D" will say she was annoyed to no end, I know it meant a lot to her, to feel that someone was looking out for her. It meant the world to me knowing that she wasn't alone.

It's not that everyone said cruel things to us or about us, although some did. There were no real "sides" to take except that suddenly, we were alone. I understood . . . what in the world do you say to someone whose life is undergoing such chaos? Jae went about experiencing as much of life as she could, while "D" and I were left picking up the pieces. I felt shunned from the life I had led. Knowing there were people close to us, who didn't tell me about Jae's other life, left me very distrustful. In trying to see things from Jae's point of view, a different world was opening up for me and I was very unhappy over it.

I met friends of Jae's that, I'm sure were very nice people, but I saw them as entities that were taking Jay away from me. I attended a support meeting with her and was crushed with emotion for the despair and loneliness that I saw. People were truly suffering because of identity issues within themselves. She paid much more attention to these new friends, than she did for her own family. I now believe that no one would go through all of this on purpose. Jae felt she had no choice in the matter of sexual identity – her outward appearance needed to match the inner picture she had of herself. Meanwhile, I was trying to stay grounded for *our* daughter (and honestly, I started thinking of her as *my* daughter) because Jae wasn't there for us anymore. I couldn't rely on her. And truthfully, when Jae was physically with us, there was a barrier present as well. I'm sure that I'm as responsible for that barrier as Jae is, but I started taking over the role of mom *and* dad because Jae wasn't really interested in playing the role of dad. And I was *VERY* adamant that "D" had only one "mom". I know that bothered Jae as she really didn't like being referred to as "Dad" anymore.

Although I knew that I could not stay legally married to a woman forever, there was no real hurry on my part to end things. It was already over. Financially, Jay was trying to hold onto the truss business while beginning her life as Jae. As long as we remained married, part of Jae's health needs would be covered by my insurance, and I felt that was the best and only real way that I could support my husband. I also believed that as soon as my husband's sexual orientation was "corrected", inevitably, our marriage would no longer be recognized as such. I didn't want anyone else putting words in my mouth or saying "she thinks . . ." I foolishly thought, that because we were still married, Jae would honor his promises to me and would eventually be thinking about our future as well. Therefore, I agreed to participate in the documentary, as long as they would leave "D" out of it because she did **not** want any part of it.

We had a round, outdoor pool that hadn't been set up for a few years. I was actually growing a nice bunch of tree frogs in it for my nature classes. As the filming progressed, Jae had this awesome idea that we should clean up the pool and open it for the summer. Now, summer is pretty hot and "D" loved the pool, but I knew there must be some alternative reason that Jae wanted the pool open. It turns out that it was a unique way to film us, as a family, for the documentary. I still cringe at the memory of how Jae handled the bathing suit shots and "playing" in the pool. I had agreed to open the pool for our own benefit, remembering the enjoyment we usually get out of the cool water but I didn't like being used. I asked that we only "swim" for a shooting session and not act like we were as close as we used to be. I was uncomfortable in my suit and was uncomfortable for Jae in hers, as she wore a woman's suit. It didn't matter what I said, Jae was playful and splashing on camera, having a grand old time. I don't think she even cared how uncomfortable it made me and I was angry about it for days. My limited trust in her was beginning to wane.

Another time, Jae talked "D" into getting the horses out for a shot in the documentary. Well, "D" had already stated that she wanted no part of the show but Jae wheedled and coaxed until she relented. We got the horses out for a ride, something which Jae hadn't done in years, just so that she could be seen participating with the family. I could tell that "D" was upset by the way she sat the horse. It was just so one sided, that it made me sick.

That year of transition was hell. "D" would yell at me for using that word, but it was. In fact, the next four years were dreadful, but there were so many blessings that kept my soul afloat . . . somehow. There were unexpected cards from family encouraging me. There were sympathetic hugs and smiles from people I wasn't even close to, that gave me a lift. My daughter and I grew closer as we relied on each other daily. I have the utmost respect for my husband, in finally standing up for himself and for physically, going through everything he did. I said my peace for the interviews and I supported Jae as much as I could. Although I have met some great people that have gender issues, I have no intention of telling their stories or of influencing opinions. Jae opened up a world that I didn't want to be part of. There is so much pain for some people and there are real worries of diseases and tragedies. We all share the need to be ourselves, and to feel accepted and loved. Life is not fair and fair is not equal. We all face our own demons and we all have to make our own choices. We do what we feel we have to do and we are the ones who have to live with it. The past has ultimately shaped the present. And the dust settles . . .

28

It turns out that Jay had been wearing those "Halloween" clothes and shoes to other towns and cities, posing as a woman for years. The phone call to my parents that day, was just the tip of the iceberg. According to Jae, those locked cupboards/closets in all of the businesses, were hidden items of Jay's that he didn't want discovered. But on the other hand, how much stress did I waste over being jealous over other women? I wonder if it had seemed like a game to Jay; how close was I getting before I found out the truth? Was he waiting for me to discover his secret myself? Maybe it was my fault that I didn't discover the truth sooner?!

There are definitely times during that year that I cannot forget. The first meeting at school among people I have known for years - I wasn't even hearing the speaker. I was looking at each person, wondering what secret they were hiding in their lives. Thinking back, maybe we should have taken an ad out in the paper, to let everyone know at the same time. It seemed to me, at the time, that everyone knew about Jae's transition but didn't know what to say, so they said nothing. Actually, there are times, even now, that I find people I have worked with for years, that *don't* know my history at all. On the other hand, some never spoke to me again!

But there were some who tried to change Jae's mind. Those people, Jae tried to win over to her "side", or she just wrote them off. Still fewer tried to accept the changes and remain friends with both of us. It turned out, that we each were able to hang on to some treasured friends that loved us both, no matter what. My friend, Deb, was one of these people. Although she didn't agree with Jae's decisions, she tried to keep an open line of communication with both of us and really tried to remain neutral. Unfortunately, Jae was not interested in neutrality . . . it was her way or the highway. Deb remains a precious ally for me and we have shared tears of sorrow and joy throughout our lives. I'm grateful that she calls me friend.

During that year of transition, I was faced with people who mocked the situation, people that scorned us, people that traveled the course with us and people that prayed for us. My brother's family, whom I had hoped would help keep "D" grounded in family, needed to take care of their own health issues. They were beset with problems which, naturally, took precedent. My sister, bless her heart, was there as a shoulder to cry on, a tormentor against what she saw as my weaknesses, a babysitter for "D", and a steadfast anchor of reality. She never remarried so there was no male influence for her girls. Although my Dad's health was failing, he tried so hard to be there for us. He never put down Jae in my hearing and he became the father figure for "D" and her cousins. He actually took "D" and one cousin to the "Daddy/Daughter Dance" at school. He was so proud to be with two of his girls that night! We have pictures showing the girls all dressed up and Grandpa standing proudly between them. I think he somehow knew, he wouldn't get the chance to participate in our lives as much anymore. I cherish those memories and I know the girls do too.

It seems that God had His own way to keep me on track, and He put people in my life that helped point the way. Even the sermon one Sunday, was pointed directly at me and boy, I felt it burn. The passages teaching about husbands loving their wives and the commitment they should have to each other, hit me like a rock. I realized that I could not support Jae entirely in this. It was sucking me dry. I needed to be strong for "D's" sake and I could not just ride the wave anymore. I decided then and there, just how far I could follow my husband and started making choices to benefit us. Acting on those choices was difficult, because Jae was a master manipulator.

29

"D" and I became inseparable. Not that I was trying to keep her tied to me, it's just that I seemed to be the anchor for her. Six months into the transitional year, after watching her "daddy" pretend to be a girl, "D" asked me, "When is daddy changing back?" As gently as possible, I tried to explain to her, that daddy was happy as he was and would not be changing back. She never asked anything about it again but she became more withdrawn and seemed happiest with her cousins or her horses.

Our 4H club became our therapy. We were able to upgrade animals from a pony to an Arabian gelding just "D's" size. He was a bit aloof, like her and she honed her riding skills on him. He got her attention, both good and bad, until they bonded, the best of buds. He remains the love of her life, well, besides the dog. That dog!!!

We've always had a dog, or two, okay - or three. Truthfully, after "D" was born, we had three and inherited two more. We loved them as our children, until "D" came along. This was another great reason to get out of the mobile home we were in and finish the house. I had to put the Christmas tree in the playpen to keep everything away from the "kids"! In my mind's eye, I can still see "D" riding her red tricycle through the unfinished hallways of our house trailing 5 dogs behind her. Sadly, she doesn't remember helping her dad paint the walls. I wish I had left her hand prints all over her room. I also remember the day I was so tired I fell asleep on "D's" unfinished bedroom floor. She was playing in the room with me and as I lay there, half asleep, I felt soft fingers on my face. I awoke to the fact that she had colored my face half green with her markers! Fortunately, it wasn't permanent. Precious stuff I will always remember and treasure.

Anyway, I'm not sure why but Jae decided to promise "D" a puppy during this emotional year. Of course, "D" was extremely excited and couldn't wait to pick one out. At that time, we only had one dog that had been a stray and nobody liked him but me. Some friends of Jae's had an English Springer Spaniel that was pregnant, so Jae brainwashed "D" into wanting one of these puppies SO badly that I couldn't say no. I say brainwashed because "D" had been talking about another kind of dog and she knows I like mutts. I'm sorry, but I cannot recommend the English Springer as a good, family dog. I really can't believe I didn't kill that dog during the first two years of her life! I've learned to love her now, but as a puppy she got the brunt of my anger and emotional turmoil, especially while the filming crew was in our home. She got into *everything* and chewed it to pieces. She urinated on *everything* and whenever someone came into the house, she peed on the floor. Apparently, this is not that unheard of in the dog world but it was a constant source of irritation to me, since the film crew had set up in our home toward the end of Jae's year. It seemed that everyone was coming in and going out all the time (going being the key word here). And, of course, after helping "D" pick out the puppy, and after buying it for her, guess who had the job of taking care of the cute, new puppy? Yup!!

We lost that dog in the past year but I still talk to her. She's buried on our land next to a variety of past, treasured pets and I visit the cemetery often for respite. I've added another rescue to our menagerie – a 100 lb. beast that is as naughty as he is cute. "D" says she hates my dog so perhaps we're even. I know she doesn't, just like she knows I actually loved her dog, but wow, it was a long time before that dog charmed her way into my heart. In my mind's eye, I still see her foraging inside a huge, empty bag of Pedigree for the very last crumb of food. Only her tail showed. She was always hungry.

I do believe that part of the reason I disliked that dog, was because she represented the point of money to me. It was during the final half of Jae's time frame, that the business was obviously starting to falter. After 9/11, the economy changed dramatically anyway and we hung on as long as we could. However, once the film crew came, Jae was off reinventing her life and being interviewed. She left a lot of the business details to the foreman and me. Although I knew how to physically build the trusses, I had no idea of how to design them - that was Jae's major input into the company. And Jae had other things on her agenda.

30

From what I could see, Jae was in her glory. She was being recognized for who she thought she was; she was getting lots of attention from the film crew, and she stopped caring about what it was doing to the rest of us. At least that's how it looked from our end. She got new clothes and a new hairdo. I had shared the details of my life with a few people at work, in order to have an explanation for some of my behavior. I continued to feel anxious around others and had a very hard time being in a closed room, or even sitting within a large group of people. I still prefer the end of a line of chairs. I get really uptight when surrounded in a room. On a good note, Jae had stopped coming to school conferences which made everyone there (and me), more comfortable.

There were quite a few people in our circle of friends and family that tried to advise me during this time. I allowed Jae to stay at home and complete this change in her life because I truly felt led to do it. Jae even built an apartment in the basement for herself, thinking it would be an ideal place to let herself go without having pre-teen eyes watching everything. It was a private place for Jae to meet with people in her life that were not involved with me. It was my hope to preserve the relationship "D" had with her dad, while shielding her from as much of the "extra stuff" as I could. The upcoming surgery was not explained to "D" by me, as she was not asking questions about it. Jae, on the other hand, wanted her to know everything and we had many a heated argument over it. I knew that Jae wanted "D" to accept the new person that Jae was, but I did not want Jae to thrust her abnormal ideas into "D's" head as being normal. Jae's new life was indeed abnormal to what our life had been, and "D" could see that for herself. "D" would have to make up her own mind about gender issues but gender issues were not the only thing that was keeping them apart. We didn't appear as a family anymore. We didn't fit the picture of a complete family anymore. Jae was trying too hard and not giving "D" the time to adjust. *My* acceptance was limited. Jae would have to earn any true acceptance from "D", on her own.

Jay had always needed me to listen to him. He felt the need to be so explanatory that it border-lined pushy. Remember the holes in the wall? What turned out to be the biggest problem with all of Jay's gender issues, was that it couldn't be done quietly. Jay was not that kind of person! From Jay's point of view, nothing in the world had changed. He was looking out from the same perspective, expecting everything else to remain the same. It was one person trying to make one, simple, physical change but the mower deck of his life seemed to reach infinity. It involved every single aspect of our lives and it was extremely difficult to handle. There was shrapnel and damage everywhere, both inside and out, visible and not, to all of us.

There were people giving me advice that I knew truly cared about me. There were people that I knew were on Jae's "side", advising me. Once the documentary came out, there were people I'd never heard of, calling to talk to me. I had to start acting on the conviction that I felt in my heart. It was in direct conflict with the part of me that wanted to support my husband.

I truly believe there are birth defects that are not recognized as such. How much better to be able to visualize and admit our "flaws" so that we can accept them, get help if possible, and go on with our lives! I have a friend that lost her leg . . . the physical and mental support she needed was obvious. I deal with mentally impaired students. Whole classrooms are designed to help them. The blind and deaf can learn through adaptation; factories are set up to make special equipment for those in need. I'm a woman . . . I don't even have to think about it. It's just part of me. I feel that gender issues are such a personal part of us that we tend to steer away from people with ideas and problems far from our own scope of reality. How can you fix or sympathize with something that you can't see? How can you explain something to someone, if they don't want to see it?

I feel people confuse the terms "gay, lesbian, transgender" as being sexual preferences. It was explained to me (I think I got it straight}, that these terms are describing how the person perceives himself. How they view life after that, is their own choices. Their sexual preferences are their own choices. How they act upon their own choices, is the "sticky" part. I believe in a morality about sexual choices. For my own part, I can only answer for myself and act on faith.

I must confess, I think I could have handled it better, if it hadn't gotten so messy. In my naivety, I tended to believe everything I was told. Jae said we would stick together. She still loved me. Nothing would change. But I would hear her on the phone with her friends, laughing and giggling, over situations that were way beyond me. She started sounding like the teenager in the family. I overheard her say things like, "I can't wait to finally be with a man." She showed me a magazine that was covering her "story". She was so proud of it and she bragged about the pictures and the comments. Well, her comments said that she was not a lesbian and that she couldn't wait to be a woman because she had needs . . . I'm paraphrasing but that is how I read it. I remember the comments that Jay had made, about the fun of being a hooker, and I realized the time would come when Jae would leave. So, I tried to prepare myself for the inevitable.

31

Jae never did live in the apartment she had built in our basement. She refused to move out of our bedroom, so I did. I couldn't remain sleeping in bed with her next to me. My own heart was in mourning over the loss of my husband, and grief brings with it, its own needs. I read a book in college, about a death in the family, and I remembered the sexual agony that the main character went through when her husband unexpectedly died. Because I could no longer have sex with my husband (in my mind), that is, of course, all my body yearned for. That part of grief was explained in college but it never hit home until I felt it. I also never expected the shock that hit me when I saw my husband fully "dressed" for the first time.

Being a builder, my husband's company would participate at the local Homebuilder shows. Jae pleaded with me to go and help represent the company that final year. She fully expected to be able to maintain the business. She said we had to have a united front. I truly believed she may have needed my help to set up the computer presentations and decorations. Besides, I'd always helped in the past. Stupid me! I said I would make an appearance. "D" and I helped prepare the displays. Jae had wanted a "Key West" theme as a layout for her booth and I was curious to see how it all turned out. She even had a palm tree and various island props.

Instead of going directly to the booth, I stopped short of it and watched from a distance. I cannot begin to describe my complete and utter shock in seeing Jae, entirely at ease, flirting with the potential customers that came to her booth. She looked amazing . . . her hair was curled pretty, she had heels, a skirt, nylons, makeup. You would NEVER have known she was physically still a guy. I thought I was going to pass out watching her. It hit me like a brick that the confidence she was showing, had not been acquired in a short year. This was the "other" person who had been present in our marriage. This was the person that had lied to me, manipulated me, haunted me, used me and was still doing all those things. Yet, somehow, this was the person I had learned to love as well. I began to see Jae as the selfish person she was. There would be no room in her life for "D" and I, once she was "complete".

I was unaware that my uncle was attending the builders show that night. As I was watching Jae, my uncle was watching me and I know I wouldn't have managed to escape the building that night, if he hadn't come over and hugged me to give me support. I made a mad dash to my car and fell to my knees on the pavement beside the car door. As I finally broke down, all I could do was gasp for air and sob. My heart was breaking and I didn't know how to go on. I don't know how long I sat there, praying for strength and composure, but that prayer became my daily ritual as I tried to maintain a "normal" existence within such a critical time. I also pulled out a poster that I had on my wall as a kid . . . The Desiderata. It spoke words of hope to me and the first line quieted my aching soul: "Go placidly amid the noise and haste, and remember what peace there may be in silence".

32

The film crew did an excellent job. I'm not going to comment on them much, as I said my piece/peace for the movie. They edited my words as they saw fit but were kind enough to leave me my interview tapes in case "D" would ever want to know more about that time in our lives. I still have not seen the entire movie. I've only watched part of it once, to see my dad and hear his voice again. The only thing I want to relay about the filming, is how disappointed I was about the fact that the advertisement about the movie showed a picture of "D". Her picture was on one of those entertainment shows that exaggerate everything and make big deals about nothing. To say the least, I was furious! A photographer had taken a shot of "D's" school pictures that were on the mirror in my bathroom. My trust in the film crew and my husband went out the window. By that time, my dad had retained an attorney for us and she did an amazingly fast job of getting that segment off the air. We were under the impression that only one of "D's" classmates made a reference to it, and it was entirely out of context. Unfortunately, there was more of an impact at school than we'd realized. Quite recently, "D" has hinted of more incidents, but she still refuses to expand on them.

Once again, I felt crushed. I had really tried to recognize the importance of this surgery for Jae. The symbolism of our marriage vows and rings, seemed of no importance to Jae and therefore lost any meaning for me. In an effort to show my support, I had taken my engagement ring to a jewelers and had them design a new ring around the stone for Jae. I had hoped Jae would comprehend the meaning behind my efforts; I had intended for it to represent a new beginning for her, but include memories for the family she was part of as well. It was meant to be something special, as I knew that she liked jewelry. I think she liked it but it meant more to the production company for their movie. The diamond wasn't very big and it had absolutely no meaning for me anymore but, in retrospect, I wish I had kept it for "D".

Jae's surgery was scheduled around the time of our local 4H fair. At least, that is when she had some pre-surgery work done. I had borrowed my Dad's cell phone while we camped at the fairgrounds and I can remember listening to Jae on the phone at night. Since Jae wanted to share everything (perhaps no one else would listen to her), I tried to at least let her talk. She ranted on and on, about how the doctor said she had some kind of hepatitis and she didn't know what she was going to do if it held up her scheduled surgery. She had no idea of the panic she put me through, on behalf of myself and "D"! Hepatitis was no laughing matter. It really *was* a very self-centered time in Jae's life. Her need to become herself took precedent over all of her actions. I don't think she ever thought of the repercussions for us – I really don't think she could. Blessedly, her health scare had no impact on us.

Fortunately, there were no complications for the scheduled surgery and she gleefully flew off to California with her girlfriend along to help in recovery. I refused to go. Jae drove my car while her friend rode in the front passenger seat so they could talk. I rode in the back so that I could drive home with the car. It was quite an emotional ride for me. I rode to the airport in silence, listening to the excited voices in the front seat. They spoke of new clothes, new shoes, palm trees, guys . . . We stopped for gas and Jae asked her friend if she wanted anything from the station. I kind of waited, expecting her to ask me as well. But she got out of the car without a second thought, and it dawned on me, that this was the essence of my life with Jae. I don't think she even remembered I was there.

Jae called me from California, now and then, to tell me how things were going: all the details. She'd found a women's shoe store that handled larger sizes and was able to buy heels for a very reasonable price, so she had ordered several pair. I cringed at all of the money she was spending but she said don't worry about it. Ha! She contacted me before, and after surgery as well. She sent out birth certificates stating the day of her surgery and the birth of a girl. She also, later, had her birth certificate changed to reflect her proper gender. She was so excited and I was happy for her. She wanted to change "D"'s birth certificate, to show Jae's new name, but I wouldn't consider it. I was beginning to find my voice.

33

When Jae came back from California, it was pretty clear that she was not going to be content here anymore. She was busy with new friends. She had meetings. Business failed; we had lost most of the big equipment (dump truck, bobcat, etc.) and I was not the easy, pushover I had always been. I was trying to prepare myself for that time when Jae would leave for good. I knew she would.

Apparently, Jae felt that the business would survive given enough time to adjust to the outward change in the owner. At some point, she even talked the bank into giving her more money, on top of what she had borrowed from my dad! She was really convincing. Obviously, they couldn't say no either. She decided to get out of the picture for a while, to let things settle. She lined up work for herself down south, and made stockholders of the workers to promote the feeling of stability. She felt she could draw the blueprints from anywhere and the crew could run the shop here in her absence. Although I get the sequence of things mixed up in my mind, I do remember that the foreman broke his leg about this time as well. For some reason, Jae did not want to be seen at her construction company and couldn't participate in the construction of the last big order of trusses. My family came to the rescue again. I read the diagrams, measured and cut the wood. My dad and uncle helped to clamp the plates on the trusses while the injured foreman helped wherever he could. It was a labor of love. It was love for each other that showed in the support my family gave to me. It was love lost, as shown by the fact it was the last physical effort on my part to support my husband. It was love ... finally, sincerely, irrevocably, done. Ironically, I fell off the trailer as we were loading the trusses onto the trailer and I dealt with shoulder pain for years.

When Jae left to find herself down south, she consistently called to share her experiences with me. I took my wedding band off completely, to remind myself that I was alone but I realized that I needed to keep track of Jae. This job down south was temporary and she was expecting to come home. I was led to believe that life would calm down with her gone and that when she came home, it would be easier for her to pick up the pieces of business as Jae.

I cannot recount Jae's trip south although she informed me of most of the hurdles. It is her story to tell, but I will share how abused I felt hearing all about it. Instead of a profound thanks for my efforts, I was regaled with horror stories that I didn't need to hear. Somehow, she made each encounter, each element of the trip, pertinent to her new identity. There was too much emotion ... she was still trying to draw me into her life. I was trying to cut the ties. In order to keep my sanity, I wrote letters to myself at night. Most of those letters were lost when my computer crashed, but I've included one that was saved, to show the stress I was under. Please keep in mind that this letter was not intended for any purpose but to vent my frustration at the time:

January 29, 2003 (12:08 AM)

Well, I don't know what to think. In fact, I can't really think about it at all. (Jae) called this evening and began her usual chit-chat. She had another really lousy day ... went out for drinks with workers after work and watched them get drunk. Apparently the new head guy got talking and talked himself into quitting on the spot! The conversation went on but soon switched to the topic she has broached for weeks now ... we were really going to have to talk in February.

I was getting pretty tired of hearing that because it usually means bad things for me. She's been saying it since she went back to Florida after Christmas. Every single phone call, usually every other day or more, would eventually wind down to "we're really going to have to talk". Well, I guess this was the day.

(Jae) just confessed to having slept with a guy she had met in Florida. She started the conversation by reminding me that I had requested that we be honest with each other. I did say that. I fully expected that the time would come for (Jae) to experience all the things she had missed out on in life. However, I did not imagine that it would be so soon or that she would do this while we were still married. Granted, the "marriage" had been over for a while but I have always been concerned with the image of life, love, marriage, etc. that we were teaching (D) and I was simply stunned!

(Jae) stated that the real reason that she had one more interview was so that is was recorded for posterity in her "story". I wonder how she broached the subject to (them)? I asked her a few questions and just listened . . . she said it was someone she had met, who she thought was important to her and that cared about her. Unfortunately, (Jae) seems to have been used. She sounded like a teenager and I told her that she sounded just like a "girl", not a 47 year old with much more experience than that! I am unsure of what to do. I do not want to remain married to a woman, I do not want to remain married to someone who sleeps around, I do not want my daughter to see how little her daddy thinks of our "marriage" or of me. I seem to remember that this is the person who said he/she would <u>never</u> divorce me – it seems to me that he/she just did.

I asked her if it was only one time – she said yes. I asked her if he wore "protection" (thinking more of diseases) and she said "yes, of course" quite indignantly. I asked her when it was and she said, I think, just before her birthday which was January 7th. That was right after her week trip home for the holidays. She said it was "alright – not what she expected" . . . I said I didn't think I wanted all the details. She further explained that "he" was going back to his old girlfriend. No one down there knows "Jae's" past except Kathy. I wondered if (friend) found it easier to live in honesty?!

It's 12:30 – I need to get some sleep. Perchance to dream . . . Help!!

34

Life seemed much quieter with Jae out of the house. It seemed that "D" and I could breathe a little easier, although there were obvious issues still along the way. With the film crew gone and me back to work, I was left holding the bag in many ways. "D" was unable to make any choices for herself. She continued to be withdrawn and relied on me to make choices for her. Having come from a history of others making choices for me, I realized that I needed some help. Our attorney suggested speaking to a guidance counselor and recommended one close by. I was also more involved in speaking with the attorney about protecting ourselves.

I have to say that I had the best attorney possible. My dad found her and retained her services for me. Surprisingly, she had some previous experience with cases like this one, and I appreciated her expertise in handling it. She was also a nurse so she had expertise in many of the issues at hand. She advised me that things would get ugly and we tried to stay ahead of the game with Jae.

Realizing that a divorce was inevitable, I started voicing questions to Jae. It was impossible to think that the business could survive without the boss, and it couldn't. In short, really short time, the business failed and went into foreclosure. Whatever Jae was making out of state, continued to cover our mortgage at home as well as her living expenses. However, she was making hints that it was becoming harder for her to do this. I was forwarding everything business related to her at her new location. I refused to be involved anymore.

About six months after she left, Jae announced that she would be coming home for a visit. I tried to prepare her that we would need to talk about the future, and she assured me that we would. I had checked online about how to get a cheap, quick, mutually agreed upon divorce and had paperwork for her to look at. I was really hopeful that we could amicably end this marriage that was only on paper anyway. My folks had given me the land to build on but, being a dutiful wife at the time, I had wanted it in both our names. I was hoping that she would sign off from the house so that we would be able to save it for "D". Obviously, personal finances were heading south as well, and I wanted to be able to preserve our home front for "D's" *emotional* welfare, as well as mine. Jay had built it for us and I truly didn't think she wanted to lose it to foreclosure as well. "D" needed her room, her therapy animals, everything she had known and wasn't changing, around her. I knew that she was hurting inside but she wasn't talking about it. Besides, this was home.

During the course of this "visit", Jae did everything *but* sit down with me and talk. She actually hand built an enclosed trailer from scraps and started packing things into it to take back with her. In reality, it was pretty impressive. But, it was all under the pretext that she would be needing these things in her job. I didn't believe it. She took tools and supplies from the pole barn and had people over, helping her load things into the trailer. She spent time visiting people she hadn't seen in a while and seemed to be happy. Since most of this was done while I was working, I really didn't realize everything she was doing. Jae told me that she wanted to spend her last, full day with us and I gathered my information together for that time. I guess I still wanted to trust that she cared about us.

That last day home was not at all what I had hoped for. Jae wheedled her own plans into the day so that, instead of spending time alone, we went on a picnic with "D" and filled the day with other fun things for her. Every time I brought up the future, my comments were shot down and the conversation changed. It was pretty obvious that Jae had no intention of allowing me time to talk, so I had to be blunt and asked her to look at the paperwork I had for a divorce. I tried to explain that it was to protect our investment of the home and that it certainly should be no surprise to her that I would not want to stay married to a woman. She had even said as much months before in the magazine article about herself.

Jae was out of control when she heard the word divorce. She started yelling at me about trying to steal the property and would not even look at the paperwork. I truly think she had expected us to hit bottom with her . . . then she wouldn't be alone. She accused me of trying to take her daughter away from her and pulled a really bad girlish fit. She didn't care that we could lose the house - she fully expected my dad to bail me out. She was throwing things into the trailer right up until the time that she pulled out. Unfortunately, none of this was lost on "D".

I do not need to go into all the details of the divorce. In fact, from my initial knowledge of my husband's transgenderism, it took 4 years to get divorced. I think most of our conflicts during the proceedings were customary for divorce. Although some of Jae's activities worked against her claim for custody, her gender identity had little to do with the length of time it took. And, I still have not paid off the attorney. In actuality, my dad had agreed to pay the cost but everything changed when my dad's condition worsened.

When our business failed, and the land went into foreclosure, it was finally brought to my attention how much my father had invested in Jae's cause. This amazing attorney did as much as she could for my entire family. She knew how the system could work to our advantage, she was compassionate to the circumstances and even intervened with Jae personally when necessary. I spent many an afternoon conversing in her office, looking over notes and court documents. This woman was my hero and I thank her from the bottom of my heart.

Anyone having to go through foreclosure, knows the anxiety involved. When you add in the stress of divorce, it's almost unbearable. The business was sold in a snow storm, for pennies on the dollar and the money was applied toward the debts of the company. Our home was listed on Jae's bankruptcy and I truly thought I was going to lose that, too. Understandably, there was nothing left to pay back my parents. My dad never spoke of it and although I have felt so tremendously burdened by that fact, there is really no appropriate word of explanation except . . . love.

35

Since I had been mailing the company information to Jae, I was not included in any paperwork or information, so I felt the need to separate myself from the business. During the course of those 4 years, I had been having my income taxes done as "married filing separately" which helped alienate me from whatever Jae was doing. I notified the commercial bank that I would not be responsible for anything Jae had done with them. As expected, Jae stopped paying the mortgage when she filed bankruptcy. Jae always had a hard time holding herself in check and exploded at a court meeting, stating that she was going to make big money some day and never give any to me. She took everything she wanted from the house earlier so there wasn't a lot to fight over, except the house and custody of "D". I was able to obtain a mortgage in my name, using court ordered child support money (which I didn't get) as income and was able to buy my home back from the bankruptcy court. I am profoundly grateful to the mortgage company agents, as they handled the ugly circumstances of transferring deeds, etc., with much patience and understanding.

In the summer of 2003, my dad broke his hip and was diagnosed with bone cancer, on top of his kidney failure. The attorney was able to place a hold on the court case, so that we could deal with the more important situation. Jae knew my dad was not well but I chose not to share the seriousness of this with her. I seldom had conversations with Jae about anything else but "D" anyway. Jae had sent my dad a letter during this time that was completely inappropriate. In my mind, I felt Jae was still interfering with my life and putting a lot of expectations on my dad. Maybe I shouldn't have been so angry, since Jae had no idea my dad was so very ill, but I know that it hurt my dad. Dad did so much for Jay/Jae over the years, that I've had a hard time forgiving her of this. *Jay* had a hard time seeing things from anyone else's point of view, and it seemed that *Jae* had a hard time wearing someone else's shoes as well. It was a hurtful and selfish letter . . . especially to a dying man. My dad began cancer treatments and I didn't learn about the letter until later.

In October of that year, my dad decided he had had enough with the cancer treatments and decided to take himself off from kidney dialysis to let nature take its course. He had lost a brother and a nephew, to bone cancer and knew exactly what to expect. He didn't want to go through that and he wanted to save us from having to go through that. I remember my mom calling me at school and telling me that dad wanted to come home to die. She was very distraught and didn't know what to do. I could only tell her that it wasn't our decision to make. I was completely torn by my own emotions but I felt we don't often get to make the choice on when to let go. My dad had found a way and we couldn't take that choice away from him. I'm not sure where those words came from, but I felt that unseen, steadying hand on my shoulder. My mom asked if I could come and get them from the hospital to take them home. I said of course I would and called my sister before leaving, to let her know our plans.

The principal of the school, where I was working, took me aside and told me she understood how important it was to be there for dad. She had lost a parent under similar circumstances as well, and her sympathy was awe-inspiring. We cried with each other, over our own lost memories. She said to take as long as I needed.

I rushed out to the parking lot to grab my truck and go. I was crying uncontrollably and could hardly see through my tears. I seldom have reliable transportation and this truck was no exception. My door handle never worked and I had to leave the corner window open, in order to reach through and open the truck from the inside. I couldn't seem to get the corner window open that afternoon. Looking through the window, I could see that the edge of the window was locked!

My heart hit the pavement and I started screaming and pounding on the window in desperation. It was while I was gasping for breath, that I heard the kitten. When it registered what I was hearing, I paused long enough to turn around and consciously look for the sound. As my eyes searched around me, my thoughts finally calmed and I realized that I would be of no use to anyone, if I didn't focus. I looked high and low but the sound had stopped. There was no kitten. I sent off a quick prayer of thanksgiving, thinking that whatever it was, it had at least cleared my head. Almost as an afterthought, I gave one last push on the glass and the window easily opened. What a miracle! I was in much better shape to drive now and I hurried on my way, conscious of the fact that God had not abandoned me.

The drive home from the hospital was long. Not in distance but in memories. It was the last drive my dad took and believe me, I took our time. Once home, our lives were placed on hold, while we spent as much time as we could with mom and dad. My mom is the strongest person I know, and she tried so hard to be strong for us all. But I know of the times that she cried alone, the times that we cried together, and the times she crawled into the hospital bed with dad to cry. Love hurts!

I learned so much about life while watching my father die. This was nothing like watching my marriage die . . . this was way more crushing and meaningful! We were all fortunate to be able to live so close to my folks. I was able to work around their home and still be close enough for lunch, a story, a TV show, a phone call, or a hug. Support came from all around us. People brought us food to eat, cards and gifts for my dad (papa) and prayers for the family. We'd have daily dinners and the grandkids would meet at my folks after school. Although we tried to keep the kids on their regular routine of school, they understood that papa was going to die.

When hospice was called in, we had already moved papa's bed

to the main floor and were already physically caring for him. They left us pretty much on our own except for medications, instructions, personal care items and prayers. They were an exceptional group of people and I'm grateful to them for their service and support of us.

Papa had requested no visitors when he got home and it was very difficult to keep family away. His sister, especially, wanted to see him, but he was adamant. I got a tape recorder and recorded messages from his peers and our family. These were messages of remembrance and hope. They were messages of love and he seemed to take comfort in them. I know I did.

Again, my folks were finding ways, albeit very sad ways, to bring us all together as a family. Papa made it through Halloween. His bed was set up in the room facing the front steps, and he could watch as the kids came down to trick-or-treat. There were also baby raccoons under the stairway that came out at night and spied in his window. I took pictures of that time when Papa was last home. No one wanted to see them but I needed to freeze that time in my mind and heart. There were times that we laughed so hard we cried, and times that we sat in silence, watching a movie together. We all talked a lot because it was becoming more difficult for Papa to talk. Eventually, he was sleeping most of the time and wouldn't even take a drink of water. My dad's last words to me were an apology about leaving things undone. My heart broke as I explained to him that everything would be okay . . . no one expected more. I tried to calm his fears and read him scriptures out of the Bible, but I think it was more for my own benefit. It took both my mom and I to take care of dad's bodily needs, but each of us kids were able to find ways to give back to our parents during this time. My sister, bless her heart, was the head chef and wonder girl. My brother brought news of the business world and son talk. It was never enough but sometimes, that's all there is . . . Love.

Papa passed on Monday morning, November 10, 2003, but he had been in a coma for days. He came out of his coma the Sunday afternoon before he passed. It was just as my brother was pulling in with his family from church. My sister and her girls were there as well and it was the most moving time I can ever remember. Papa's face actually glowed with happiness. He was alert and, although he couldn't talk, he seemed to understand all that was said to him. He was "awake" for maybe an hour or so, while each person there spoke to him and told him goodbye in their own way. He focused on each one and smiled that smile of his. Shortly after the last kiss, he fell back to sleep.

Sunday night, while my mom and I were changing my dad's linen, mom threw her back out. She was sleeping on the couch and discovered that she could not stand from the pain. Our chiropractor made a house call and tried to keep mom immobile, thus easing some of the pain. On Monday morning, when Papa was gasping his last, we tried to bring his bed closer to hers. She wanted so badly to be with him. My sister and I tugged and pulled on his hospital bed, trying to roll it to hers, but we couldn't budge it. We ended up dividing; while she stayed with mom, I stayed with dad. We kept trading back and forth. It was over pretty quick.

When each of my family was saying goodbye to Papa the day before, I was observing and taking pictures. I had said goodbye to him several times before. I caught his eye and smile on Sunday but he had a gift for me the morning of his death. It took a while for everyone to be notified about Papa's passing. My brother came, hospice came, and the undertakers came.

After the men came, and removed Papa from his bed, it immediately broke apart and fell to the floor. My sister and I looked at each other and just shook our heads. We had pushed and pulled on that thing just hours before and it had stood its ground. As I thanked God for keeping that bed together, I thought I heard my dad laughing . . .

I knew that once Papa's body left the house, I wouldn't see him again. His wish had been to be cremated. I had assisted the gal from hospice in his final preparations and had combed his hair, but I just couldn't let him go. As I followed the team taking him out of the house, I was watching his face and saw it transform into youth. I know people may say I'm crazy or maybe that all bodies do that, but to me it brought a sweet feeling of peace. I didn't see my "old" dad lying there. I saw the young Navy man that my mom had fallen in love with. He was actually smiling as they were carrying him to the vehicle. I knew that Dad was in good hands.

36

Somehow, my mom survived the next few weeks until she had back surgery. She stood for the funeral, which had standing room only and tried to adjust to the empty house. My sister stayed with her many nights to assist her and to keep her company. After recovering from her back surgery, mom continued to support me in divorce proceedings. She got a job at the local supermarket, as a greeter and tried to go about living as best she could. She made some very good friends at work and she had finally found a place to use her "gift of gab" as they say. The customers looked forward to seeing her and she learned to love her job.

They say it takes at least a year of mourning before you should make any major changes in life. I think that's because you have to face each previous holiday, each special day of the year once, alone, before you can see beyond it. After 50+ years of marriage, I realized that my mom was not going to find it easy to go on. Dad was cremated and we put some of his ashes up north where we had always snowmobiled, and also into the ocean that he loved. I'm not saying that I wish Jay had ended his life, I only wish that my mourning was only for a year . . .

As previously mentioned, the divorce took four years to complete. Divorce is so humiliating at times. Jae fought me every step of the way. Although she finally signed off with a quit deed, she made everything as difficult as she could. The letters I wrote in the dead of night, to myself, were to help keep my sanity. These were heartfelt messages of anguish, anger, pain, loneliness, frustration, fear and ultimately, of love. It is very hard to let go. The home that we saw as a haven, at times, became isolation instead.

My attorney stayed one step ahead of Jae all the way. She has been a great sounding board and a truly caring friend. When Jae wanted overnight visitation, my attorney sent us to a guidance center. "D's" sessions with the counselor were a battleground for me because she would not say one word to the therapist. The woman tried playing games and making up stories. "D" loved to color and draw but wouldn't touch anything. We finally ended the visits when she locked me out of the car as I went around it to get her. I had to pull her from the car and almost carry her, in order to take her in. Interestingly, when we said she didn't have to go anymore, she started talking her head off. I think maybe there were some control issues there!

I had added counseling sessions for myself as well. This allowed me to have a professional opinion about parental visits and such during the course of the divorce case. I am forever grateful to the woman who, quite impulsively said, "I like you - you're good people". She had no idea how much I needed to hear that! Those three words, I like you, kept my head and heart above water, while the rest of my world was sinking.

I was able to get a letter from them stating that overnight visits, at least at that time, were not in "D's" best interest. When Jae wanted to claim half of the cemetery lots, which I had paid for, the attorney was able to dismiss the requests. I was so overwrought at times, that she was the voice of reason that kept me on task. Jae sent letters stating she thought our "union" was important for the sake of our daughter and maybe we should wait. My attorney saw through the smoke screen and kept me on course. Jae sent me cards and letters at the beginning of the divorce proceedings, stating what a good parent I was, how much she loved me. These changed, of course, to words of scorn and ridicule. I'm sure all of this is quite natural in divorces but I now have sympathy for all who have to face this.

When I continued the case after dad died, Jae suddenly turned greedy and tried to get anything she could out of me. She'd change her demands which would, of course, create more paperwork, stall the case, and add fees to my bill. Jae had ample opportunity to take everything she could from our home, which she did. She took everything she could out of the business before it collapsed and she left me with all the paperwork, trash, creditors, and ruin. She wanted half my retirement with the school or anything else I had of value. She demanded respect and earned none. She would not show up for court proceedings or cancel at the last minute, knowing I had to take off work in order to attend. I could not understand why Jae would want "D" to lose the home she felt secure in, the animals that were her therapy, her ability to be in 4H which was also her social therapy. She had already lost the sense of "family" like her friends all had. Our old pictures now had a flaw in them as dad wasn't really dad. How confusing it must have been for her! I admit I was confused too . . . I actually put away a lot of our pictures.

Eventually, Jae moved back into the area. In order to pick up "D" for visitation, we took turns in transportation. Jae would constantly complain about having to pick up at my mom's house. I felt my mom's home was a neutral place for "D". I did not want Jae anywhere near our house and I couldn't always be present. Jae never told "D" that she couldn't call her dad but "D" didn't know what to call her instead. Jae also complained that my mom would call for "D" out of the den saying that her "dad" was here. Jae seemed to complain about everything but in the long run, the paperwork was filed and the divorce was finalized.

In my case, I wanted the companionship of the man I married, the joy of a hug, reciprocal trust, and the reassurance of conversation. There were no winners in this case but my attorney saved as much, physically, as she could for us. She even, personally, bought Christmas gifts for "D" and myself that first year. As I said, she is a special lady and I thank God for her. The divorce papers established that I was the legal guardian and Jae had specific visitation rights should "D" *want* to go. By then, she was 15 years old and very uncomfortable with some conversations and situations that came up with Jae. The courts recognized that "D" should have a voice in her own choices. I was supposed to get continuing child support, which didn't happen often. I did what I could do, and could no longer put myself in Jay's/Jae's shoes; I accepted the shoes God gave me. They fit me the best. I am free.

37

I know that there are many people out there facing hardships in health, finances and family. It can be very hard to see things from another point of view and yet, sometimes it's the only way to keep your sanity. If there is divorce in the family, then the best way you can look at it, is from the children's point of view (if there are any). Unfortunately at times, we need to be reminded that parenting means sacrificing part of yourself. Focusing on my daughter's needs and wellbeing helped to keep me on track with the courts. While I was fighting for whatever I could salvage for her, I was escaping the reality of the loneliness that engulfed me. I can talk a good talk, but I have to admit that at times, I felt so alone that I closed myself in the car or my room and simply cried my heart out. Just because I could accept Jae's decisions for herself, it doesn't mean I agreed. My mind played so many other scenarios and possibilities that I was overwhelmed by sorrow. I realized that I had to live with my own decisions, but I was truly heartbroken over the future that was lost. I had to let go of the dreams I had held on to since I said "I do". I was so hurt that at times, I felt on the brink of a deep chasm and had to crawl back to level ground. It was also at these trying times that I felt so much anger, which was entirely misplaced. I *know* in my heart that Jay did not do all this to hurt me but I couldn't always control the natural tide of self-pity. It was at these deep, low points in my emotional life, that God placed people in my life to throw me a lifeline. Many thanks to all who uplifted my spirits with a smile, card, phone call or hug. I still have those moments of despair but the reality of blessings counterbalances the effects of feeling so alone.

38

Years ago, I was dubbed a worrywart and that is precisely what I am. I am extremely worried about money, about our mental health, about our physical health, about everything. I am learning to trust in God because He has seen me through it all; if He brought me to it, He'll certainly see me through it. I just have to let go of the reins.

I continue to feel uneasy in crowds and I have to really talk myself into saying yes to things. I am forever grateful to the people I work with. They have been very patient with my "weirdness" and try to include me in social events. I'm getting used to being the third wheel so to speak. I seldom accept invitations to activities, but I recognize that the issues are within me and I hope they never stop asking.

I still work as a paraprofessional and I've been blessed to have worked with some wonderful families in the school system. They seem to appreciate my sense of humor and dedication to my job. My positions at school bring together all my training and experiences in life, and help to bridge some of the loneliness of my days.

Honestly, I'm not sure how to continue with the phases of my life. The courts deemed that Jae had had ample time to take what she wanted from our home so I got everything that was left. This included the mess, some of which still remains today. When I finally got the divorce papers in the mail, it was a bit of a letdown. The earth didn't shake. No more shoes fell. I don't think I even shared it with anyone but close family. However, I did feel the need to buy a red bra and a chain saw. I'm not sure what that signifies?! Life is definitely a journey that changes directions. Keep the faith!

My nieces have grown into young adults that are making something of themselves. They have found wonderful young men to share their life travels with – they are happy. One is actively trying to become a mom (memories there!) and we're all praying for that to happen. She and her husband will be such loving, caring parents. The other one has seen her fair share of challenges to her body and soul. She is currently planning her wedding. I'm really proud of her, for standing up for herself and becoming who she needs to be. Her fiancé is an amazing young man that truly loves her for herself. God loves them . . . they are great examples to "D".

"D" has graduated from high school and university. There were many challenges in her education. I wanted her to attend a smaller college where she could take her horse, and participate in riding competitions. She chose to attend the State University for 4½ years and stayed in the dorms the entire time. It broke my heart that she didn't make many friends and I found it very difficult to be the sole parent. The best thing that Jae did for "D", was to get her a cell phone. I still remember the phone calls home to me: car problems, class changes, roommate issues, or simply that she couldn't understand the teacher's accent. She could have obtained a scholarship through the LGBT program. The directors simply wanted to speak to her but she chose to obtain her own financing. I think that speaks to the fact that she is her own person and wants to do things her own way. Although she has not yet found the perfect job (in her mind), she is working among children and animals. She's become certified to teach therapeutic horseback riding as well. She shares so much of herself with the students in her care; I see her growing each day. I pray God continues to strengthen her and allows her to be fulfilled in her dreams. She is a wonderful blend of Jae and me. She has her dad's quick humor and confidence in herself. I am *so* proud of her! Words can't convey what she means to me. However, I know someday, she'll need to go out on her own. I tell her that she has to take her horse with her but that's not true. I'll push her out as best as I can when the time comes.

Mom had a stroke a few years back and lives with my sister. She is unable to drive and thus lost her job, which is a heartache for her. After being laid off from her own work, my sister took on the sole responsibility of taking care of mom. It never would have worked in years past but right now, I think they are taking care of each other. It is not easy but my brother and I try to give them as much support as possible. God bless my sister for being there for family. One of my fondest things is to go visit them and see them Wii bowling together in the living room. They banter back and forth about who is the better bowler. I have much admiration for my sister and the patience she has found late in life. She has demonstrated a strength that I did not know she possessed. I admire my mom for her patience with all of us and for her ability to laugh in spite of it all. Go mom!

My brothers' boys are almost all grown . . . I cannot keep track of them as they are all involved in some kind of classes, work and sports. I cannot understand how anyone functions with more than one child . . .

Unfortunately, time has also claimed my mother-in-law. I still called her mom and I visited her in the hospital before she passed. Her funeral, which I attended with "D", was full of love and family. It was very gratifying to greet Jae's side of the family again, since I had claimed them for twenty-four years as well. Although I was uncomfortable in Jae's presence, I was able to catch up with the new additions and give comfort to family members. Mom had an unconditional mother's love and inner faith. She was a great lady and I feel honored to have called her mom.

I always wanted a lot of kids so I guess I have them through the school system. Although I've worked hard to attain the position I have, the educational system has deemed that being a para-pro is no longer a career. They have cut our hours and benefits, so making ends meet is a constant challenge. Fortunately, the students themselves remain the joy of the job, so I'm staying as long as I can. The powers that be seem to change the way we do things, but kids are kids and

I love them. I have met some heroic people in the educational field, both in the therapeutic world and the school system. There are many people that I need to thank. The Bible says to surround yourself with good people, and I have been blessed with the best. They keep me focused and give me strength. You are judged by the company you keep . . . value true friendships and be there for each other.

I would love to someday dedicate my home and acreage to be a camp where students can come out and learn what I have learned from nature: walks between the lakes, snakes under the hay, tree frogs hanging from the side of the house, deer and turkey sharing the field with the horses. Heaven! It will be with the help of God, if this dream ever comes to fruition but this time, right now, will end and I have very little control as to the outcome. Life is like that.

I don't know where God will guide me but I have faith that it will always be in my best interest to follow Him. Listen to others with your heart, and remember that you are the one that has to live with your own decisions. We are not all that different. We are, after all, humans. Make good choices and remember to forgive.

Jae . . . is still part of our lives. Much more "D's" than mine, as she still lives out of state. Jae slammed the door when she left and I've locked it. That door will remain shut, although I still miss my best friend Jay. I cannot trust my feelings for Jae. She has not earned any rights to the present or my future life. Although she continues to have health issues, I understand that she has found peace in herself and is happy. Apparently, she has also found a person that she can share her life with. "D" traveled to Florida, to be present at the wedding and had a great time vacationing with Jae and the new step-family. The wedding took place on the beach where we all have such wonderful memories from the past. I'm sure they are hoping for new, happy memories to begin. I cannot speak for her any more than that. I truly wish her happiness. I pray that her family has forgiven me, if they have felt slighted by me in the past. I am blessed with my friends and family but I still feel that Jae needs the love and support of her own family which, of necessity, leaves me out of the circle. I love them as

I love my own and I treasure many happy memories of holidays and get-togethers. Blessings to them!

I have yet to find the courage to open my heart to another should God lead me into it. I've met a few people over the past couple years, that have reminded me that I am alone by choice. I tell myself that I am content being alone and right now, that is true. I've had the opportunity to make new friends but I know that I'm much too reserved. As a mom, I feel that I have failed "D" in demonstrating to her, how to make friends. Of all things, I want her to have a full, happy life in whatever she decides to do. She has her own health issues that she is working on and I continue to be grateful for her company. I pray that God continues to guide me and I trust that He is not finished with me yet!

I am leaning on the shoulder of Christ. At present, my work is my therapy and my joy. I'm having to slow down a bit because they keep moving the bases further away in soft ball (I catch for the church team) but I'll play as long as they'll let me. God reminds me in little ways that life is better when I bring Him with me in whatever I do. I realize that I still have trust issues and I have to learn to let go of all the baggage of life. I have to learn how to make friends again. I just bought a hamster. When "D" leaves, the house will be empty. Pray for me. Maybe I'll get another dog . . .?!

Printed in the United States
By Bookmasters